Racial Discrimination

Other books in the Issues on Trial series:

Racial Discrimination

Mitchell Young, Book Editor

GREENHAVEN PRESS

An imprint of Thomson Gale, a part of The Thomson Corporation

THOMSON
™
GALE

Detroit • New York • San Francisco • San Diego • New Haven, Conn.
Waterville, Maine • London • Munich

Bonnie Szumski, *Publisher*
Helen Cothran, *Managing Editor*
Scott Barbour, *Series Editor*

For more information, contact:
Greenhaven Press
27500 Drake Rd.
Farmington Hills, MI 48331-3535
Or you can visit our Internet site at http://www.gale.com

LIBRARY OF CONGRESS CATALOGING-IN-PUBLICATION DATA

Racial discrimination / Mitchell Young, book editor.
   p. cm. -- (Issues on trial)
   Includes bibliographical references and index.
   0-7377-2787-X (library binding : alk. paper)
   1. Race discrimination--Law and legislation--United States--Cases.
2. Race discrimination--United States. 3. Segregation--United States. 4. Hate crimes--United States. 5. Affirmative action programs--United States. I. Young, Mitchell. II. Series.
   KF4755.A7R35 2006
   345.7308'73--dc22
                                                                        2005055092

#6269717 4

Printed in the United States of America
10 9 8 7 6 5 4 3 2 1

Contents

Chapter 1: Upholding Legalized Segregation

Chapter 2: Outlawing School Segregation

Since the early 1990s schools have become more segregated as parents have had more school choices. This situation threatens to undo the decades of progress after the *Brown* decision.

Chapter 3: Declaring Hate Crime Laws Constitutional

Chapter 4: Legalizing Racial Preferences in College Admissions

Permitted in College Admissions
Sandra Day O'Connor

Having a diverse student body from varying ethnic backgrounds is a compelling state interest. Race can be considered a factor in admissions in order to attain that goal.

The University of Michigan Law School's admission system is a barely disguised racial balancing system and is in violation of the Fourteenth Amendment. White and Asian students are severely disadvantaged under this system.

Diversity programs inevitably lead to attempts to have proportional representation of ethnic groups in the student body. Such programs go against the American tradition of individual rights.

Admissions officials use the *Grutter* decision to devise policies that appear constitutional while actually discriminating in favor of minorities.

Grutter will allow greater numbers of minorities to receive a higher education and occupy positions of leadership in business, politics, the military, and other sectors of American society.

Foreword

The U.S. courts have long served as a battleground for the most highly charged and contentious issues of the time. Divisive matters are often brought into the legal system by activists who feel strongly for their cause and demand an official resolution. Indeed, subjects that give rise to intense emotions or involve closely held religious or moral beliefs lay at the heart of the most polemical court rulings in history. One such case was *Brown v. Board of Education* (1954), which ended racial segregation in schools. Prior to *Brown*, the courts had held that blacks could be forced to use separate facilities as long as these facilities were equal to that of whites.

For years many groups had opposed segregation based on religious, moral, and legal grounds. Educators produced heartfelt testimony that segregated schooling greatly disadvantaged black children. They noted that in comparison to whites, blacks received a substandard education in deplorable conditions. Religious leaders such as Martin Luther King Jr. preached that the harsh treatment of blacks was immoral and unjust. Many involved in civil rights law, such as Thurgood Marshall, called for equal protection of all people under the law, as their study of the Constitution had indicated that segregation was illegal and un-American. Whatever their motivation for ending the practice, and despite the threats they received from segregationists, these ardent activists remained unwavering in their cause.

Those fighting against the integration of schools were mainly white southerners who did not believe that whites and blacks should intermingle. Blacks were subordinate to whites, they maintained, and society had to resist any attempt to break down strict color lines. Some white southerners charged that segregated schooling was *not* hindering blacks' education. For example, Virginia attorney general J. Lindsay Almond asserted, "With the help and the sympathy and the love and re-spect of the white people of the South, the colored man has risen under that educational process to a place of eminence and respect throughout the nation. It has served him well." So when the Supreme Court ruled against the segregationists in *Brown*, the South responded with vociferous cries of protest. Even government leaders criticized the decision. The governor of Arkansas, Orval Faubus, stated that he would not "be a party to any attempt to force acceptance of change to which the people are so overwhelmingly opposed." Indeed, resistance to integration was so great that when black students arrived at the formerly all-white Central High School in Arkansas, fed-eral troops had to be dispatched to quell a threatening mob of protesters.

Nevertheless, the *Brown* decision was enforced and the South integrated its schools. In this instance, the Court, while not settling the issue to everyone's satisfaction, functioned as an instrument of progress by forcing a major social change. Historian David Halberstam observes that the *Brown* ruling "deprived segregationist practices of their moral legiti-macy.... It was therefore perhaps the single most important moment of the decade, the moment that separated the old or-der from the new and helped create the tumultuous era just arriving." Considered one of the most important victories for civil rights, *Brown* paved the way for challenges to racial seg-regation in many areas, including on public buses and in res-taurants.

In examining *Brown*, it becomes apparent that the courts play an influential role—and face an arduous challenge—in shaping the debate over emotionally charged social issues. Judges must balance competing interests, keeping in mind the high stakes and intense emotions on both sides. As exempli-fied by *Brown*, judicial decisions often upset the status quo and initiate significant changes in society. Greenhaven Press's Issues on Trial series captures the controversy surrounding in-fluential court rulings and explores the social ramifications of such decisions from varying perspectives. Each anthology highlights one social issue—such as the death penalty, students' rights, or wartime civil liberties. Each volume then focuses on key historical and contemporary court cases that helped mold the issue as we know it today. The books include a compendium of primary sources—court rulings, dissents, and immediate reactions to the rulings—as well as secondary sources from experts in the field, people involved in the cases, legal analysts, and other commentators opining on the implications and legacy of the chosen cases. An annotated table of contents, an in-depth introduction, and prefaces that overview each case all provide context as readers delve into the topic at hand. To help students fully probe the subject, each volume contains book and periodical bibliographies, a comprehensive index, and a list of organizations to contact. With these features, the Issues on Trial series offers a well-rounded perspective on the courts' role in framing society's thorniest, most impassioned debates.

Introduction

The roots of racial discrimination in America go back to the very beginnings of European settlement. By 1619 African slaves were being imported to supply the labor needs of southern colonies. For the next two and a half centuries, throughout the colonial era and in the early decades of the independent United States, blacks (and only blacks) could be legally enslaved. The legacy of slavery would lead to a profound racial divide in America. While other racial groups were also discriminated against, racial discrimination by whites against blacks was the most deeply entrenched and difficult to resolve.

While the defeat of the South in the Civil War (1861–1865) ended slavery, it did not end the racial discrimination against blacks. However, three changes to the Constitution, the so-called Civil War Amendments, did give African Americans the rights of citizens. The Thirteenth Amendment ended slavery. The Fourteenth Amendment gave civil rights as full citizens to all persons born or naturalized in the United States. And the Fifteenth Amendment guaranteed all citizens the right to vote. By passing these amendments, Congress provided African Americans the means to appeal to the courts when local or state governments violated their rights.

Setbacks in the Courts

In the years after the Civil War, blacks made some progress against discrimination. Following in the wake of the constitutional amendments, Congress even passed legislation prohibiting discrimination in some types of businesses (inns and taverns) and on public means of transportation (such as trains). Unfortunately, in early decisions the Supreme Court limited the scope of the constitutional amendments and other

In the 1880s and 1890s many southern states passed discriminatory measures, which were known as Jim Crow laws. Racial segregation was ultimately deemed unconstitutional by the Supreme Court. © Bettmann/CORBIS

antidiscrimination legislation. In the Slaughterhouse Cases (1873) the Court held that the states, rather than the federal government, had jurisdiction over its citizens' civil rights. The Civil Rights Cases (1883) held that Congress lacked authority to prevent racial discrimination by private individuals or businesses.

These Supreme Court decisions were taken as a green light for both individuals and state governments to introduce discriminatory measures. In the 1880s and 1890s so-called Jim Crow laws were passed in many southern states. These laws required the segregation of the races in public places such as restaurants and hotels, on public means of transportation such as trains, and in public schools. In addition, a series of laws in the southern states gradually restricted the ability of blacks to vote. Unable to pursue their constitutional rights through the democratic process, African Americans turned once again to the courts for help.

Progress Toward Desegregation

At first blacks and their supporters were let down by the courts, including the U.S. Supreme Court. In 1896 the Court ruled in *Plessy v. Ferguson* that laws requiring racial segregation were constitutional as long as facilities for blacks and whites were of equal quality. One judge dissented, however. Justice John Harlan wrote that "there is no caste" in the United States, meaning that governments had no right to make distinctions among citizens by race. Governments at all levels— federal, state, and local—were obliged by the Constitution to ignore race. Though he did not use the phrase, Harlan's position has come to be known as advocating a "color-blind" Constitution.

While the *Plessy* decision was a setback, groups pursuing civil rights continued their battle in the courts. With time, Supreme Court decisions whittled away at segregation. For instance, the Court ruled in *McLaurin v. Oklahoma* (1950) that requiring a black student in a graduate program to eat at different times and to receive separate instruction than whites violated the right to an equal education. However, Jim Crow policies were still considered constitutional until the 1954 *Brown v. Board of Education* decision, which outlawed discrimination in public schools.

New Challenges in a Diverse Society

Outlawing segregation did not end America's racial difficulties, however. The oppression that blacks and others had experienced over the centuries left a large gap in amount of wealth, educational attainment, and social status between blacks and whites. The federal and state governments, as well as educational institutions and private companies, have instituted programs to overcome these historical disadvantages. These programs are known collectively as "affirmative action."

At universities affirmative action programs give blacks and other disadvantaged groups extra consideration when applying for admission. In the workplace they are goals and guidelines that seek to attain a certain percentage of minority employees in an organization. In instituting these programs, governments, educational institutions, and companies seek to make up for past discrimination. More recently, such programs have gone beyond the effort to make up for past discrimination; they now focus on attaining a workforce or student body that reflects the racial diversity of American society.

The Supreme Court has upheld affirmative action in two notable cases. In *The University of California Regents v. Bakke* (1978), a divided Court ruled that race and ethnic background could be used in an attempt to bring about a diverse student body. And in *Grutter v. Bollinger* (2003), in a five to four decision, the justices held that states have a compelling interest in ensuring that all ethnic groups are represented in institutions, such as law schools, that educate the future leaders of society.

Many people object to affirmative action policies, however. Opponents believe that affirmative action does not fit with Harlan's vision of a society that does not make distinctions based on race. These critics believe that while well intentioned, such distinctions violate Americans' right to equality before the law. Opponents have had some success at blocking affirmative action programs. In the states of California and Washington they succeeded in bringing propositions to the ballot that effectively outlaw such programs. Race-neutral policies are required for college admissions, government employment, and awarding of government contracts. A similar measure is planned in Michigan, the state were the *Grutter* case originated.

Free Speech Versus Racial Tolerance

Affirmative action and diversity programs are not the only area of controversy involving race. The courts have also had to deal with the tricky issue of hate crimes legislation. Afraid that racially inflammatory speech and race-based crime de-

Students rally in support of affirmative action in Washington, D.C. The Supreme Court upheld affirmative action in the 2003 Grutter *decision to ensure ethnic diversity in educational institutions.* Alex Wong/Getty Images

stroy the fabric of a diverse society, local officials, state legislatures, and the U.S. Congress have all passed hate crime laws. These laws allow prosecutors to seek extra severe punishments against those convicted of committing a crime motivated by racial discrimination. Opponents of these laws worry that by punishing motivation, rather than action, they actually penalize people for their beliefs and thoughts. Thus the laws could undermine people's freedom to believe whatever they choose and to speak openly about their views, eroding their First Amendment guarantee of free speech.

The Supreme Court has attempted to protect freedom of speech while also allowing prosecutors to attach enhanced penalties to some violent crimes. In *R.A.V. v. St. Paul* (1992) it ruled that laws that restrict speech or the display of offensive symbols violate people's First Amendment right to free expression. However, it also ruled in *Wisconsin v. Mitchell* (1993) that violence that is racially motivated can be punished more severely than similar crimes in which no racial bias is evident.

While the vast majority of Americans agree that racially based crimes should be punished, some people worry that punishing identical crimes—such as two murders—differently because of the intention of the criminal will lead to a two-tier system of justice in which some victims are more valued than others.

An Ongoing Struggle

In the attempts to prevent hate crimes—as well as the efforts to end segregation and increase the participation of blacks in society by means of affirmative action—the courts have played a major role. This anthology seeks to explore these issues by looking at four of the major Court decisions related to racial discrimination in America: *Plessy v. Ferguson* (1896), *Brown v. Board of Education* (1954), *Wisconsin v. Mitchell* (1993), and *Grutter v. Bollinger* (2003). By presenting the Supreme Court's decisions, the views of dissenting justices, and commentary on the impact of the cases, *Issues on Trial: Racial Discrimination* sheds light on the long, painful, ongoing struggle to realize the ideal of American equality.

CHAPTER 1

Upholding Legalized Segregation

Chapter Preface

Case Overview: *Plessy v. Ferguson* (1896)

Immediately following the Civil War, the Republican Party–dominated federal government undertook measures to guarantee newly freed African Americans' civil and political rights. Chief among these were the "Civil War Amendments": The Thirteenth Amendment abolished slavery; the Fourteenth Amendment guaranteed due process and equal protection under the law to all citizens; and the Fifteenth Amendment guaranteed voting rights. With federal troops stationed in the South to ensure that their rights were protected, blacks made a degree of progress. Some state legislatures in the South passed laws promoting civil rights and prohibiting discrimination against the freedmen. Blacks, working with their white Republican allies, were able to gain real political power in many southern states.

However, after federal troops were withdrawn from the South in 1877, white southerners managed to wrest back some political control. As they grew more powerful, they began to pass laws detrimental to blacks' interests. In particular, southern state legislatures began to approve measures to segregate blacks from whites in public accommodations such as restaurants and hotels, in schools, and on means of transport such as buses and railroads.

Louisiana followed this general pattern. After the Civil War its legislature had passed laws that ensured blacks' right to equal treatment not only in public areas but also in any private businesses licensed by the state. By 1873 laws prohibited all discrimination in public or private accommodation. But as in other states, segregation soon returned as white southerners retook political control. In 1890 the Louisiana state legislature passed a law requiring that railways provide separate cars for blacks and whites and that anyone with any discernible "African blood" was required to ride in the car designated for black people.

African Americans and Creoles (Louisianans who traced their ancestry back to French and Spanish settlers and African slaves) set about to challenge the law. They set up a *Comité des Citoyens* (Committee of Citizens), composed of leading black and Creole citizens of New Orleans, in order to fight the railroad segregation law. The group, led by New Orleans businessman and lawyer Louis A. Martinet, hired a white lawyer, Albion Tourgée, to represent them. The strategy was to claim that segregation violated the Fourteenth Amendment's right to due process under the law.

In 1892 Tourgée, along with another white lawyer, James C. Walker, had Homer Plessy, a shoemaker who was seven-eighths white and one-eighth black, board a train of the East Louisiana Railroad. Plessy notified the train conductor that he was black and proceeded to take a seat in the whites-only car of the train. When asked to sit in the car reserved for blacks, Plessy refused to leave his seat. He was subsequently arrested and put in jail.

The *Plessy* case worked its way through the court system and finally arrived at the U.S. Supreme Court. In 1896 the Court ruled that the law requiring segregation of trains traveling within Louisiana was constitutional. The majority opinion, written by Justice Henry B. Brown, held that the framers of the Fourteenth Amendment had meant to give blacks political equality but not social equality. As long as blacks were accommodated equally, as supposedly was the case with the white and black railway cars, then the Louisiana law did not violate the Fourteenth Amendment simply by preventing commingling of the races.

As a result of *Plessy*, segregation became more entrenched in the South. Assured of their constitutionality, more states passed laws requiring segregation of public transport, accommodation, and schooling. At the same time, African Americans and others organized the National Association for the Advancement of Colored People to begin a decades-long struggle to fight these laws. After a series of small victories, they were finally able to overturn *Plessy* in *Brown v. Board of Education* (1954).

> "We cannot say that a law which au-
> thorizes or even requires the sepa-
> ration of the two races in public
> conveyances is unreasonable."

The Court's Opinion: Forced Segregation Is Constitutional

Henry B. Brown

Henry B. Brown was a Supreme Court justice from 1890 to 1906. He authored more than 450 majority opinions, many supporting private property rights and open competition in economic matters. He is most famous today, however, for his majority opinion in Plessy v. Ferguson.

In his majority opinion, Justice Brown quickly dismisses the arguments of Homer Plessy's lawyers that legal segregation is similar to slavery or servitude and thus violates the Thirteenth Amendment to the Constitution. He also concludes that a law requiring segregation on railways does not violate the Fourteenth Amendment's guarantee of equal treatment under the law. That amendment was intended to enforce political equality, not social equality. Therefore, as long as blacks and whites are equal under the law, federal courts are not authorized to interfere with "reasonable" state legislation mandating the separation of the races in public accommodations. As Louisiana law provides for equal opportunity for travel, but only reflects a social convention that races should be separated, Justice Brown finds that it is reasonable and therefore legal under the Constitution.

T his case turns upon the constitutionality of an act of the General Assembly of the State of Louisiana, passed in

Henry B. Brown, majority opinion, *Plessy v. Ferguson,* U.S. Supreme Court, 1896.

1890, providing for separate railway carriages for the white and colored races.

Provisions of the Law

The first section of the statute enacts

that all railway companies carrying passengers in their coaches in this State shall provide equal but separate accommodations for the white and colored races by providing two or more passenger coaches for each passenger train, or by dividing the passenger coaches by a partition so as to secure separate accommodations: *Provided*, That this section shall not be construed to apply to street railroads. No person or persons, shall be admitted to occupy seats in coaches other than the ones assigned to them on account of the race they belong to.

By the second section, it was enacted

that the officers of such passenger trains shall have power and are hereby required to assign each passenger to the coach or compartment used for the race to which such passenger belongs; any passenger insisting on going into a coach or compartment to which by race he does not belong shall be liable to a fine of twenty-five dollars, or in lieu thereof to imprisonment for a period of not more than twenty days in the parish prison, and any officer of any railroad insisting on assigning a passenger to a coach or compartment other than the one set aside for the race to which said passenger belongs shall be liable to a fine of twenty-five dollars, or in lieu thereof to imprisonment for a period of not more than twenty days in the parish prison; and should any passenger refuse to occupy the coach or compartment to which he or she is assigned by the officer of such railway, said officer shall have power to refuse to carry such passenger on his train, and for such refusal neither he nor the railway company which he represents shall be liable for damages in any of the courts of this State.

The third section provides penalties for the refusal or neglect of the officers, directors, conductors, and employees of railway companies to comply with the act, with a proviso that "nothing in this act shall be construed as applying to nurses attending children of the other race." The fourth section is immaterial. . . .

Segregation Is Not Slavery

The constitutionality of this act is attacked upon the ground that it conflicts both with the Thirteenth Amendment of the Constitution, abolishing slavery, and the Fourteenth Amendment, which prohibits certain restrictive legislation on the part of the States.

1. That it does not conflict with the Thirteenth Amendment which abolished slavery and involuntary servitude, except as a punishment for crime, is too clear for argument. Slavery implies involuntary servitude—a state of bondage; the ownership of mankind as a chattel, or at least the control of the labor and services of one man for the benefit of another, and the absence of a legal right to the disposal of his own person, property and services. This amendment was said in the *Slaughterhouse Cases* [1873] to have been intended primarily to abolish slavery as it had been previously known in this country, and that it equally forbade Mexican peonage or the Chinese coolie trade when they amounted to slavery or involuntary servitude, and that the use of the word "servitude" was intended to prohibit the use of all forms of involuntary slavery, of whatever class or name. It was intimated, however, in that case that this amendment was regarded by the statesmen of that day as insufficient to protect the colored race from certain laws which had been enacted in the Southern States, imposing upon the colored race onerous disabilities and burdens and curtailing their rights in the pursuit of life, liberty and

property to such an extent that their freedom was of little value; and that the Fourteenth Amendment was devised to meet this exigency.

So, too, in the *Civil Rights Cases* [1883], it was said that the act of a mere individual, the owner of an inn, a public conveyance or place of amusement, refusing accommodations to colored people cannot be justly regarded as imposing any badge of slavery or servitude upon the applicant, but only as involving an ordinary civil injury, properly cognizable by the laws of the State and presumably subject to redress by those laws until the contrary appears. "It would be running the slavery argument into the ground," said Mr. Justice [Joseph P.] Bradley,

> to make it apply to every act of discrimination which a person may see fit to make as to the guests he will entertain, or as to the people he will take into his coach or cab or car, or admit to his concert or theatre, or deal with in other matters of intercourse or business.

A statute which implies merely a legal distinction between the white and colored races—a distinction which is founded in the color of the two races and which must always exist so long as white men are distinguished from the other race by color—has no tendency to destroy the legal equality of the two races, or reestablish a state of involuntary servitude. Indeed, we do not understand that the Thirteenth Amendment is strenuously relied upon by the plaintiff in error in this connection.

Due Process Is Preserved

2. By the Fourteenth Amendment, all persons born or naturalized in the United States and subject to the jurisdiction thereof are made citizens of the United States and of the State wherein they reside, and the States are forbidden from making or enforcing any law which shall abridge the privileges or immuni-

ties of citizens of the United States, or shall deprive any person of life, liberty, or property without due process of law, or deny to any person within their jurisdiction the equal protection of the laws.

The object of the amendment was undoubtedly to enforce the absolute equality of the two races before the law, but, in the nature of things, it could not have been intended to abolish distinctions based upon color, or to enforce social, as distinguished from political, equality, or a commingling of the two races upon terms unsatisfactory to either. Laws permitting, and even requiring, their separation in places where they are liable to be brought into contact do not necessarily imply the inferiority of either race to the other, and have been generally, if not universally, recognized as within the competency of the state legislatures in the exercise of their police power. The most common instance of this is connected with the establishment of separate schools for white and colored children, which has been held to be a valid exercise of the legislative power even by courts of States where the political rights of the colored race have been longest and most earnestly enforced.

Reasonable Regulation

It is claimed by the plaintiff in error that, in any mixed community, the reputation of belonging to the dominant race, in this instance the white race, is property in the same sense that a right of action or of inheritance is property. Conceding this to be so for the purposes of this case, we are unable to see how this statute deprives him of, or in any way affects his right to, such property. If he be a white man and assigned to a colored coach, he may have his action for damages against the company for being deprived of his so-called property. Upon the other hand, if he be a colored man and be so assigned, he has been deprived of no property, since he is not lawfully entitled to the reputation of being a white man.

In this connection, it is also suggested by the learned counsel for the plaintiff in error that the same argument that will justify the state legislature in requiring railways to provide separate accommodations for the two races will also authorize them to require separate cars to be provided for people whose hair is of a certain color, or who are aliens, or who belong to certain nationalities, or to enact laws requiring colored people to walk upon one side of the street and white people upon the other, or requiring white men's houses to be painted white and colored men's black, or their vehicles or business signs to be of different colors, upon the theory that one side of the street is as good as the other, or that a house or vehicle of one color is as good as one of another color. The reply to all this is that every exercise of the police power must be reasonable, and extend only to such laws as are enacted in good faith for the promotion of the public good, and not for the annoyance or oppression of a particular class. . . .

So far, then, as a conflict with the Fourteenth Amendment is concerned, the case reduces itself to the question whether the statute of Louisiana is a reasonable regulation, and, with respect to this, there must necessarily be a large discretion on the part of the legislature. In determining the question of reasonableness, it is at liberty to act with reference to the established usages, customs, and traditions of the people, and with a view to the promotion of their comfort and the preservation of the public peace and good order. Gauged by this standard, we cannot say that a law which authorizes or even requires the separation of the two races in public conveyances is unreasonable, or more obnoxious to the Fourteenth Amendment than the acts of Congress requiring separate schools for colored children in the District of Columbia, the constitutionality of which does not seem to have been questioned, or the corresponding acts of state legislatures.

Social Equality Must Be Voluntary

We consider the underlying fallacy of the plaintiff's argument to consist in the assumption that the enforced separation of the two races stamps the colored race with a badge of inferiority. If this be so, it is not by reason of anything found in the act, but solely because the colored race chooses to put that construction upon it. The argument necessarily assumes that if, as has been more than once the case and is not unlikely to be so again, the colored race should become the dominant power in the state legislature, and should enact a law in precisely similar terms, it would thereby relegate the white race to an inferior position. We imagine that the white race, at least, would not acquiesce in this assumption. The argument also assumes that social prejudices may be overcome by legislation, and that equal rights cannot be secured to the negro except by an enforced commingling of the two races. We cannot accept this proposition. If the two races are to meet upon terms of social equality, it must be the result of natural affinities, a mutual appreciation of each other's merits, and a voluntary consent of individuals. As was said by the Court of Appeals of New York in *People v. Gallagher*

> this end can neither be accomplished nor promoted by laws which conflict with the general sentiment of the community upon whom they are designed to operate. When the government, therefore, has secured to each of its citizens equal rights before the law and equal opportunities for improvement and progress, it has accomplished the end for which it was organized, and performed all of the functions respecting social advantages with which it is endowed.

Legislation is powerless to eradicate racial instincts or to abolish distinctions based upon physical differences, and the attempt to do so can only result in accentuating the difficulties of the present situation. If the civil and political rights of both races be equal, one cannot be inferior to the other civilly or politically. If one race be inferior to the other socially, the Constitution of the United States cannot put them upon the same plane.

> *"State enactments regulating the enjoyment of civil rights upon the basis of race . . . can have no other result than to render permanent peace impossible."*

Dissenting Opinion: The *Plessy* Decision Will Lead to Racial Conflict

John Harlan

John Harlan was a justice of the U.S. Supreme Court from 1877 until 1911. He was raised in Kentucky and was therefore perhaps more familiar with problems of race relations than his fellow Supreme Court justices, who were northerners.

Harlan dissented vigorously from the majority opinion in Plessy, *which upheld the constitutionality of state laws requiring racial segregation. In the following excerpt from his dissent, Harlan holds that the ruling violates the Constitution's requirement that all citizens be treated equally under the law. While segregation laws pretend to require that segregated facilities be equal for both races, Harlan argues, the very institution of segregation is designed to mark blacks as inferior and subordinate to whites. Harlan predicts that the majority's opinion in* Plessy *will lead to more oppressive legislation against blacks in the South—a prediction that subsequently proved accurate.*

T he white race deems itself to be the dominant race in this country. And so it is, in prestige, in achievements, in education, in wealth, and in power. So, I doubt not, it will con-

John Harlan, dissenting opinion, *Plessy v. Ferguson,* U.S. Supreme Court, 1896.

tinue to be for all time, if it remains true to its great heritage, and holds fast to the principles of constitutional liberty. But in view of the Constitution, in the eye of the law, there is in this country no superior, dominant, ruling class of citizens. There is no caste here. Our constitution is color-blind, and neither knows nor tolerates classes among citizens. In respect of civil rights, all citizens are equal before the law. The humblest is the peer of the most powerful. The law regards man as man, and takes no account of his surroundings or of his color when his civil rights as guaranteed by the supreme law of the land are involved. It is therefore to be regretted that this high tribunal, the final expositor of the fundamental law of the land, has reached the conclusion that it is competent for a state to regulate the enjoyment by citizens of their civil rights solely upon the basis of race.

The Majority's Decision Is Harmful

In my opinion, the judgment this day rendered will, in time, prove to be quite as pernicious as the decision made by this tribunal in the Dred Scott Case.[1]

It was adjudged in that case that the descendants of Africans who were imported into this country, and sold as slaves, were not included nor intended to be included under the word 'citizens' in the constitution, and could not claim any of the rights and privileges which that instrument provided for and secured to citizens of the United States; that, at the time of the adoption of the Constitution, they were 'considered as a subordinate and inferior class of beings, who had been subjugated by the dominant race, and, whether emancipated or not, yet remained subject to their authority, and had no rights or privileges but such as those who held the power and the government might choose to grant them.' The recent amendments of the Constitution [i.e., the Thirteenth, Fourteenth,

1. In the *Dred Scott* case (1857), the Supreme Court ruled that black slaves were not entitled to any rights, including the right to sue for their freedom if brought to a free state. The case is widely thought to be a cause of the Civil War.

and Fifteenth], it was supposed, had eradicated these principles from our institutions. But it seems that we have yet, in some of the states, a dominant race,—a superior class of citizens,—which assumes to regulate the enjoyment of civil rights, common to all citizens, upon the basis of race. The present decision, it may well be apprehended, will not only stimulate aggressions, more or less brutal and irritating, upon the admitted rights of colored citizens, but will encourage the belief that it is possible, by means of state enactments, to defeat the beneficent purposes which the people of the United States had in view when they adopted the recent amendments of the Constitution, by one of which the blacks of this country were made citizens of the United States and of the states in which they respectively reside, and whose privileges and immunities, as citizens, the states are forbidden to abridge. Sixty millions of whites are in no danger from the presence here of eight millions of blacks. The destinies of the two races, in this country, are indissolubly linked together, and the interests of both require that the common government of all shall not permit the seeds of race hate to be planted under the sanction of law. What can more certainly arouse race hate, what more certainly create and perpetuate a feeling of distrust between these races, than state enactments which, in fact, proceed on the ground that colored citizens are so inferior and degraded that they cannot be allowed to sit in public coaches occupied by white citizens? That, as all will admit, is the real meaning of such legislation as was enacted in Louisiana.

Equality Will Bring Peace and Security

The sure guaranty of the peace and security of each race is the clear, distinct, unconditional recognition by our governments, national and state, of every right that inheres in civil freedom, and of the equality before the law of all citizens of the United States, without regard to race. State enactments regulating the enjoyment of civil rights upon the basis of race, and cunningly devised to defeat legitimate results of the [Civil] war, under the pretense of recognizing equality of rights, can have no other result than to render permanent peace impossible, and to keep alive a conflict of races, the continuance of which must do harm to all concerned. This question is not met by the suggestion that social equality cannot exist between the white and black races in this country. That argument, if it can be properly regarded as one, is scarcely worthy of consideration; for social equality no more exists between two races when traveling in a passenger coach or a public highway than when members of the same races sit by each other in a street car or in the jury box, or stand or sit with each other in a political assembly, or when they use in common the streets of a city or town, or when they are in the same room for the purpose of having their names placed on the registry of voters, or when they approach the ballot box in order to exercise the high privilege of voting.

A Brand of Servitude

If evils will result from the commingling of the two races upon public highways established for the benefit of all, they will be infinitely less than those that will surely come from state legislation regulating the enjoyment of civil rights upon the basis of race. We boast of the freedom enjoyed by our people above all other peoples. But it is difficult to reconcile that boast with a state of the law which, practically, puts the brand of servitude and degradation upon a large class of our fellow citizens,—our equals before the law. The thin disguise of 'equal' accommodations for passengers in railroad coaches will not mislead any one, nor atone for the wrong this day done.

The result of the whole matter is that while this Court has frequently adjudged, and at the present term has recognized the doctrine, that a state cannot, consistently with the Constitution of the United States, prevent white and black citizens, having the required qualifications for jury service, from sitting in the same jury box, it is now solemnly held that a state may prohibit white and black citizens from sitting in the same passenger coach on a public highway, or may require that they be separated by a 'partition' when in the same passenger coach. May it not now be reasonably expected that astute men of the dominant race, who affect to be disturbed at the possibility that the integrity of the white race may be corrupted, or that its supremacy will be imperiled, by contact on public highways with black people, will endeavor to procure statutes requiring white and black jurors to be separated in the jury box by a 'partition,' and that, upon retiring from the court room to consult as to their verdict, such partition, if it be a movable one, shall be taken to their consultation room, and set up in such way as to prevent black jurors from coming too close to their brother jurors of the white race. If the 'partition' used in the court room happens to be stationary, provision could be made for screens with openings through which jurors of the two races could confer as to their verdict without coming into personal contact with each other. I cannot see but that, according to the principles this day announced, such state legislation, although conceived in hostility to, and enacted for the purpose of humiliating, citizens of the United States of a particular race, would be held to be consistent with the Constitution.

Forced Separation Inconsistent with Personal Liberty

I am of opinion that the state of Louisiana is inconsistent with the personal liberty of citizens, white and black, in that state, and hostile to both the spirit and letter of the Constitution of the United States. If laws of like character should be enacted in the several states of the Union, the effect would be in the highest degree mischievous. Slavery, as an institution tolerated by law, would, it is true, have disappeared from our country; but there would remain a power in the states, by sinister legislation, to interfere with the full enjoyment of the blessings of freedom, to regulate civil rights, common to all citizens, upon the basis of race, and to place in a condition of legal inferiority a large body of American citizens, now constituting a part of the political community, called the 'People of the United States,' for whom, and by whom through representatives, our government is administered. Such a system is inconsistent with the guaranty given by the Constitution to each state of a republican form of government, and may be stricken down by congressional action, or by the courts in the discharge of their solemn duty to maintain the supreme law of the land, anything in the Constitution or laws of any state to the contrary notwithstanding.

For the reason stated, I am constrained to withhold my assent from the opinion and judgment of the majority.

> *"The prime essential of all citizen-*
> *ship is equality of personal right and*
> *the free and secure enjoyment of all*
> *public privileges."*

Segregation Denies Blacks Liberty and Equality

Albion W. Tourgée

Albion W. Tourgée was a lawyer who traveled in the South dur-
ing Reconstruction (1865–1879). His law practice specialized in
helping newly freed African Americans exercise their civil rights.
Because of his success, he was chosen by black leaders in New
Orleans to take up the case against an 1890 law requiring blacks
in Louisiana to use segregated cars when traveling by train.

In this selection from his brief for the Supreme Court in
Plessy v. Ferguson, *Tourgée attacks segregation by noting that*
the Fourteenth Amendment to the Constitution gives blacks full
equality of citizenship both in the United States as a whole and
in each state. This status as citizens also implies that African
Americans are entitled to personal liberty, to be treated equally,
and to "the Pursuit of Happiness." Segregation violates these
principles because it puts blacks in an inferior position. Rather
than being free citizens they are now marked out by the law for
special treatment. Tourgée also attacks the reasonableness of seg-
regation. If the state can segregate black people, he contends, it
can make any sort of distinctions between its citizens merely on
the whim of the legislature. He takes this argument to the ex-
treme, noting that a state legislature might think to segregate
redheaded people or demand that blacks and whites walk on

Albion W. Tourgée, brief of the plaintiff, *Plessy v. Ferguson,* U.S. Supreme Court, 1896.

separate sides of the street. Tourgée holds that any legal distinc-
tions based on race (what Tourgée calls "assortment") are un-
constitutional, as they deprive blacks of the liberty guaranteed
them by the Fourteenth Amendment.

T he Court will take notice of the fact that, in all parts of the country, race-intermixture has proceeded to such an extent that there are great numbers of citizens in whom the preponderance of the blood of one race or another, is impossible of ascertainment, except by careful scrutiny of the pedigree. As slavery did not permit the marriage of the slave, in a majority of cases even an approximate determination of this preponderance is an actual impossibility, with the most careful and deliberate weighing of evidence, much less by the casual scrutiny of a busy [railroad] conductor.

Who Is Black?

But even if it were possible to determine preponderance of blood and so determine racial character in certain cases, what should be said of those cases in which the race admixture is equal. Are they white or colored?

There is no law of the United States, or of the State of Louisiana defining the limits of race—who are white and who are "colored" ? By what rule then shall any tribunal be guided in determining racial character? It may be said that all those should be classed as colored in whom appears a visible admixture of colored blood. By what law? With what justice? Why not count every one as white in whom is visible any trace of white blood? There is but one reason to wit, the domination of the white race. Slavery not only introduced the rule of caste but prescribed its conditions, in the interests of that institution. The trace of color raised the presumption of bondage and was a bar to citizenship. The law in question is an attempt to apply this rule to the establishment of legalized caste-distinction *among citizens.*

It is not consistent with reason that the United States, having granted and bestowed *one equal citizenship* of the United States and prescribed *one equal citizenship in each state*, for all, will permit a State to compel a railway conductor to assort them arbitrarily according to his ideas of race, in the enjoyment of chartered privileges.

Segregation Violates Personal Liberty

The Plaintiff in Error [Homer Plessy], also insists that, even if it be held that such an assortment [separation] of citizens by race in the enjoyment of public privileges, is not a deprivation of liberty or property without due process of law, it is still such an interference with the personal liberty of the individual as is impossible to be made consistently with his rights as an equal citizen of the United States and of the State in which he resides.

What are the rights, "privileges and immunities of a citizen of the United States?" Previous to the adoption of this section [the Fourteenth Amendment] of the Constitution they were very vague and difficult of definition. Now they include all "the rights, privileges and immunities" *of a citizen of a State*, because that citizenship is made incidental to and coextensive with *national* citizenship in every State; and the United States guarantees the full enjoyment of both. It is evident that National citizenship *plus* State citizenship covers the whole field of individual relation, so far as the same is regulated or prescribed by law. All the rights, "privileges and immunities," which *can attach* to the individual as a part of the body-politic, are embraced either by the relation of "Citizen of the United States" or by the relation of *citizen*"of the *State* in which he may reside." The United States having granted *both* stands pledged to protect and defend both.

This provision of Section I of the Fourteenth Amendment, *creates* a *new* citizenship of the United States embracing new rights, privileges and immunities, derivable in a *new* manner, controlled by *new* authority, having a *new* scope and extent, dependent on national authority for its existence and looking to national power for its preservation.

Citizenship Means Equality

The prime essential of all citizenship is *equality* of personal right and the *free* and secure enjoyment of all public privileges. These are the very essence of citizenship in all free governments.

A law assorting the citizens of a State in the enjoyment of a public franchise on the basis of race, is obnoxious to the spirit of republican institutions, because it is a legalization of *caste*. Slavery was the very essence of caste; the climax of unequal conditions. The citizen held the highest political rank attainable in the republic; the slave was the lowest grade of existence. ALL rights and privileges attached to the one; the other had *no legal rights,* either of person or property. Between them stood that strange nondescript, the "free person of color," who had such rights only as the white people of the state where he resided saw fit to confer upon him, but he could neither become a citizen of the United States *nor of any State*. The effect of the words of the XIVth Amendment, was to put *all* these classes on the *same level of right,* as *citizens;* and to make this Court the final arbiter and custodian of these rights. The effect of a law distinguishing between citizens as to race, in the enjoyment of a public franchise, is to legalize caste and restore, in part at least, the inequality of right which was an essential incident of slavery.

State Has No Right to Label Citizens

The gist of our case is the unconstitutionality of the assortment; not the question of equal accommodation; that much, the decisions of the court give without a doubt. We insist that the State has no right to compel us to ride in a car "set apart" for a particular race, whether it is as good as another or not. Suppose the provisions were that one of these cars should be painted white and the other black; the invidiousness of the distinction would not be any greater than that provided by the act.

But if the State has a right to distinguish between citizens according to race in the enjoyment of public privilege, by compelling them to ride in separate coaches, what is to prevent the application of the same principle to other relations? Why may it not require all red-headed people to ride in a separate car? Why not require all colored people to walk on one side of the street and the whites on the other? Why may it not require every white man's house to be painted white and every colored man's black? Why may it not require every white man's vehicle to be of one color and compel the colored citizen to use one of different color on the highway? Why not require every white business man to use a white sign and every colored man who solicits customers a black one? One side of the street may be just as good as the other and the dark horses, coaches, clothes and signs may be as good or better than the white ones. The question is not as to the *equality* of the privileges enjoyed, but *the right of the State to label one citizen as white and another as colored* in the common enjoyment of a public highway as this court has often decided a railway to be.

Neither is it a question as to the right of the common-carrier to distinguish his patrons into first, second and third classes, according to the accommodation paid for. This statute is really a restriction on that right, since the carrier is thereby compelled to provide two cars for each class, and so prevented from making different rates of fares by the expense which would be incurred by a multiplicity of coaches. In fact, its plain purpose and effect is to provide the white passenger with an exclusive first class coach *without requiring him to pay an extra fare for it. . . .*

All Blacks Have the Right to Pursue Happiness

The Declaration of Independence, with a far-reaching wisdom found in no other political utterance up to that time, makes the security of the individual's right to "the pursuit of happiness," a prime object of all government. This is the controlling idea of our institutions. It dominates the national as well as the state governments. In asserting national control over both state and national citizenship, in appointing the boundaries and distinctive qualities of each, in conferring on millions [of blacks] a status they had never before known and giving to every inhabitant of the country rights never before enjoyed and in restricting the rights of the states in regard thereto,—in doing this were the people consciously and actually intending to protect this right of the individual to the pursuit of happiness or not? If they were, was it the pursuit of happiness by all or by part of the people which they sought to secure?

If the purpose was to secure the unrestricted pursuit of happiness by the four millions then just made free, now grown to nine millions, did they contemplate that they were leaving to the states the power to herd them away from her white citizens in the enjoyment of chartered privilege? Suppose a member of this court, nay, suppose every member of it, by some mysterious dispensation of providence should wake tomorrow with a black skin and curly hair—the two obvious and controlling indications of race—and in traveling through that portion of the country where the "Jim Crow[1] Car" abounds, should be ordered into it by the conductor. It is easy to imagine what would be the result, the indignation, the protests, the assertion of pure Caucasian ancestry. But the conductor, the autocrat of Caste, armed with the power of the State conferred by this statute, will listen neither to denial or protest. "In you go or out you go," is his ultimatum.

1. Segregation laws became commonly referred to as "Jim Crow."

What humiliation, what rage would then fill the judicial mind! How would the resources of language not be taxed in objurgation! Why would this sentiment prevail in your minds? Simply because you would then feel and know that such assortment of the citizens on the line of race was a discrimination intended to humiliate and degrade the former subject and dependent class—an attempt to perpetuate the caste distinctions on which slavery rested—a statute in the words of the Court "tending to reduce the colored people of the country to the condition of a subject race."

Because it does this the statute is a violation of the fundamental principles of all free government and the Fourteenth Amendment should be given that construction which will remedy such tendency and which is in plain accord with its words. Legal refinement is out of place when it seeks to find a way both to avoid the plain purport of the terms employed, the fundamental principle of our government and the controlling impulse and tendency of the American people.

> *"The historical oppression of African Americans in the United States would have been far less pervasive had . . . the 1896 views of Justice John Harlan prevailed."*

Plessy Was a Major Setback for Black Civil Rights

A. Leon Higginbotham Jr.

Justice John Harlan, who served on the Supreme Court from 1877 to 1911, was often in dissent from the majority opinion of the Court. In the Plessy *case he was the lone justice who disagreed with the Court's decision. He held that no state law could legally create distinctions based on race. However, many present-day scholars have become critical of Harlan's opinion, especially his statement that the white race was "the dominant race" in the United States.*

In the following excerpt A. Leon Higginbotham Jr. defends Justice Harlan. Harlan's opinion in Plessy, *according to Higginbotham, was correct both in legal terms and in moral terms. If a majority of the Court had adopted Harlan's views rather then the legal standard of "separate but equal," Higginbotham believes, African Americans would have continued the steady progress they had made since the end of the Civil War. Instead,* Plessy *gave free reign to segregationists, leaving a legacy of second-class citizenship that blacks would have to fight the better part of six decades to overturn.*

Higginbotham is Public Service Professor of Jurisprudence at the John F. Kennedy School of Government, Harvard University.

A. Leon Higginbotham Jr., *Shades of Freedom: Racial Politics and Presumptions of the American Legal Process*. New York: Oxford University Press, 1996. Copyright © 1996 by A. Leon Higginbotham Jr. Reproduced by permission of the publisher.

He has written many works on race and law, including In the Matter of Color *and* Shades of Freedom.

B y any fair evaluation of his substantive opinions, Justice John Marshall Harlan was one of the ten or twelve truly great justices to have ever served on the Court. He served on the Supreme Court from 1877 to 1911. When one compares his views with those of his colleagues and contemporaries of the late nineteenth century, Justice Harlan seems omniscient and heroic. There is no doubt that the status and daily lives of African Americans during the twentieth century would have been far better if the majority of the Supreme Court in 1896 had adopted the constitutional views expressed in Justice Harlan's powerful dissent. Nevertheless, for the "purists" who choose to use a twentieth-century lens to examine someone who primarily was a nineteenth-century jurist, flaws can be found in even his most memorable dissent. From my perspective, it is more fair to compare Justice Harlan with his judicial contemporaries of 1896 than to expect of him the more expansive democratic insights that were exemplified decades after his death by luminaries such as Chief Justice Earl Warren, or Justice William Brennan and Justice Thurgood Marshall; these three justices' views reached their maturity many decades after Justice Harlan's dissent.

Dispute over Harlan's Views

The tensions as to how one should evaluate Justice Harlan are exemplified in one extraordinary nine-sentence paragraph of his several-paged dissent. For devotees of Justice Harlan, there is a tendency to focus exclusively on the last six sentences of this paragraph:

> But in view of the Constitution, in the eye of the law, there is in this country no superior, dominant, ruling class of citizens. There is no caste here. Our Constitution is color-blind, and neither knows nor tolerates classes among citizens. In

respect of civil rights, all citizens are equal before the law. The humblest is the peer of the most powerful. The law regards man as man, and takes no account of his surroundings or of his color when his civil rights as guaranteed by the supreme law of the land are involved.

Harlan's most severe critics would stress the first three sentences of the same paragraph, which may dilute or minimize the egalitarian language which I have just quoted. These pivotal three sentences read as follows:

The white race deems itself to be the dominant race in this country. And so it is, in prestige, in achievements, in education, in wealth and in power. So, I doubt not, it will continue to be for all time, if it remains true to its great heritage and holds fast to the principles of constitutional liberty.

From my point of view, there is no value in having a prolonged debate on whether Justice Harlan's statement was racist or merely factual, that "The white race deems itself to be the dominant race in this country," or characterizing his apparent opinion that "it will continue to be for all time, if it remains true to its great heritage and holds fast to the principles of constitutional liberty." For me, the more important fact is that, if four other justices had adopted Harlan's view, African Americans would not have suffered from the legitimization of racism that *Plessy* caused. Justice Harlan recognized the consequences of the pernicious doctrine that the majority had approved.

He correctly observed that, in his opinion, "the judgment this day rendered will, in time, prove to be quite as pernicious as the decision made by this tribunal in the *Dred Scott* case." Harlan the former slaveowner recognized the cruelty that this opinion, where a majority of the justices were not Southerners, would impose upon African Americans. There was a pragmatic insight when Harlan commented that: "It is, therefore, to be regretted that this high tribunal, the final expositor of the fundamental law of the land, has reached the conclusion that it is competent for a State to regulate the enjoyment by citizens of their civil rights solely upon the basis of race."

Plessy Was Worse than Dred Scott

Although many lower courts had explicitly endorsed "Jim Crow segregation" prior to *Plessy*, the significance of the Supreme Court's affirmation of the doctrine of "separate but equal" in 1896 cannot be overestimated. The Court's approval was the final and most devastating judicial step in the legitimization of racism under state law. In numerous subsequent school cases, state and federal courts continued to approve racial discrimination and segregation; most of the courts or counsel of record in those cases cited or relied upon *Plessy* as support for expansive endorsements of racial subjugation.

From a race-relations standpoint, *Plessy v. Ferguson* was one of the two most venal decisions ever handed down by the United States Supreme Court. It is equalled only by the pernicious *Dred Scott v. Sandford*. Most recent scholars who have carefully studied the *Dred Scott* case have concluded that, as a matter of constitutional law, the *Dred Scott* case was wrongly decided, and that it can be explained solely by recognizing the Court's machinations to issue a political decision rather than principled adjudication. Nevertheless, in many respects, the decision of the seven justices in the majority in *Plessy v. Ferguson* was even less justifiable than the rationale proffered in *Dred Scott*. Viewing the majority opinion in *Dred Scott* in its most favorable light, one could argue that the drafters of the original Constitution had not explicitly guaranteed any citizenship rights for free African Americans and that, therefore, it was not totally irrational for the Court to reach its conclusion that an African-American man could not be a citizen of the United States. But when *Plessy* arose, it was after the Constitution had declared with specificity that African Americans were citizens of the United States and were entitled to the full privileges and immunities of citizenship. Moreover, the impact of the decision in *Plessy* was even more devastating to African Americans than that of *Dred Scott*.

Effect of *Plessy* on Black Education

Because it sanctioned the continuing oppression of African Americans, *Plessy* was one of the most catastrophic racial decisions ever rendered by an American appellate court. After *Plessy* sanctioned the concept of "separate but equal," the system in practice was separate and *un*equal. As Professor Derrick Bell notes:

> In 1915, South Carolina was spending an average of $23.76 on the education of each white child and $2.91 on that of each black child. As late as 1931, six Southern states (Alabama, Arkansas, Florida, Georgia, and North and South Carolina) spent less than one third as much for black children as for whites, and ten years later this figure had risen to only 44 percent. At the time of the 1954 decision in *Brown v. Board of Education*, the South as a whole was spending on the average $165 a year for a white pupil, and $115 for a black.

Although the Court's erroneous construction of the Fourteenth Amendment prevailed for over a half-century, the overwhelming consensus today is that *Plessy* was an untenable statement of the law that set in motion an era of oppression from which our nation still has not fully recovered. The view that *Plessy* was an untenable statement of the law is shared by jurists and lawyers with varying philosophies of federalism. From the 1970s to the 1990s, conservative Supreme Court justices and even Reagan and Bush Administration officials, as well as centrist justices of the Supreme Court declared that this case, *Plessy v. Ferguson*, was "wrong" when it was decided. Dissenting in *Fullilove v. Klutznick*, Justice Potter Stewart, joined by now-Chief Justice William Rehnquist[1] expressly

1. Rehnquist died in 2005.

stated that "*Plessy v. Ferguson* was wrong" and cited with approval Justice Harlan's famous dissent. William Bradford Reynolds, former Assistant Attorney General for Civil Rights and a noted conservative, has asserted that "racial classifications [such as those found in *Plessy*] are wrong—morally wrong—and ought not to be tolerated in any form or for any reason." In a plurality concurring opinion in *Planned Parenthood of Southeastern Pennsylvania v. Casey,* Justices [Anthony] Kennedy, [Sandra Day] O'Connor, and [David] Souter wrote, "[W]e think *Plessy* was wrong the day it was decided. . . ."

In short, had the majority of the *Plessy* Court realized, as Chief Justice Rehnquist now does, that their decision was wrong, our nation might never have needed a *Brown v. Board of Education, Missouri ex rel. Gaines v. Canada, Sweatt v. Painter,* or *McLaurin v. Oklahoma State Regents* in the field of education, because state-imposed segregation would not have been sanctioned by federal law. There also might have been no need for some of the other significant civil-rights cases that were initiated solely because the Supreme Court had held in *Plessy* that states could treat African Americans differently from how they treated the majority white population or any of the other major ethnic, religious, or national origin groups in this country. Even though many other racist forces were operating within American society—including the explicitly racist pronouncements by United States presidents, congressmen, and state governmental officials—the historical oppression of African Americans in the United States would have been far less pervasive had, in the Supreme Court, the 1896 views of Justice John Harlan prevailed.

> *"A case may be made that it was Jus-*
> *tice Brown and the* Plessy *majority*
> *who stood vindicated by the last de-*
> *cades of the twentieth century."*

The Reasoning of *Plessy* Has Not Been Overturned

Charles A. Lofgren

Charles A. Lofgren, professor of American history and politics at Claremont McKenna College in California, takes the provocative view that the central concept of Plessy v. Ferguson—*legal classification by race—is still in effect today. He notes that* Plessy *was never formally overturned in Supreme Court decisions, even in the famous* Brown v. Board of Education *school desegregation case. Lofgren argues that rather than interpreting the Constitution as color-blind and outlawing racial classification, the Supreme Court in the late 1970s started to approve racial classification for purposes such as affirmative action. In the case of* University of California v. Bakke *(1978), Justice Lewis Powell declared that race could be a factor in judging applicants to the University of California Medical School in order to boost admission of underrepresented minorities. Since then the Court has legitimized a whole series of racial classification schemes. While these actions may be intended to be benign, they nevertheless conform to the heart of Justice Henry B. Brown's reasoning in* Plessy *that legal differentiation among citizens based on race is constitutional.*

Charles A. Lofgren, *The Plessy Case: A Legal-Historical Interpretation.* New York: Oxford University Press, 1987. Copyright © 1987 by Charles A. Lofgren. Reproduced by permission of Oxford University Press, Inc.

In 1912, [Justice] Henry Billings Brown [author of the *Plessy* decision] largely conceded that John Marshall Harlan had been correct in identifying the intention behind Louisiana's separate car legislation as the degradation of blacks. By the middle of the twentieth century, Harlan seemed a prophet of the blossoming civil rights revolution, with the overturn of state-mandated school segregation in *Brown v. Board of Education* [1954] completing his constitutional vindication. Noting Harlan's vision of a color-blind Constitution, the *New York Times* editorialized after the *Brown* decision in May 1954 that "the words he used in lonely dissent . . . have become in effect . . . a part of the law of the land. . . . [T]here was not one word in Chief Justice [Earl] Warren's opinion [in *Brown*] that was inconsistent with the earlier views of Justice Harlan." Was *Plessy* vindicated?

History is seldom so neat and often more cunning. A case may be made that it was Justice Brown and the *Plessy* majority who stood vindicated by the last decades of the twentieth century. At a formal level, Chief Justice Warren failed to announce in 1954 that *Brown* had overruled the 1896 decision. Court watchers noted the omission. If not in *Brown*, some said, then the 1896 decision was overruled two years later in *Gayle v. Browder* [1956], which invalidated city-ordered segregation of buses in Montgomery, Alabama. But again the Court did not explicitly reject *Plessy*, filing only a short *per curiam* opinion [a statement made "by the Court" to clarify a point of law] that rested on *Brown*. As of mid-1986, *Shepard's Citations*, the standard "finding aid" used by lawyers to trace subsequent judicial treatment of decisions, listed no case as having overruled *Plessy*. By then, though, some judges took a different view, commenting almost in passing that the 1954 decision had overturned the earlier ruling.

More important, courts did not reject reliance on racial "facts," a central if not entirely explicit feature of Justice Brown's reasoning in *Plessy*. Nor did judges wholeheartedly embrace Justice Harlan's color-blind Constitution. The *Brown* case itself hinted that the spirit of *Plessy* survived in these regards. In upholding the finding of the federal trial court in Kansas that state-mandated segregation harmed school children, Chief Justice Warren used an argument structurally similar to the one Justice Brown had used in upholding Louisiana's conclusion that separation promoted the public's welfare. "Whatever may have been the extent of psychological knowledge at the time of *Plessy v. Ferguson*," Warren held, the trial court's factual finding was "amply supported by modern authority," a statement he then documented through his soon-controversial Footnote Eleven, which cited seven studies by social scientists. In 1896, it is true, the Court had deferred to legislative judgment about the "facts" of race, while in 1954 it deferred to a lower court's judgment, but in each instance conclusions about such "facts" entered into the reasoning. For Warren, a later critic observed, *Plessy*'s deficiency was "not that it asked the wrong questions but that it gave the wrong answers." The Chief Justice himself saw his social science authorities as important because they rebutted Justice Brown's social science.

Some Racial Classifications May Be Constitutional

In *Brown*, Warren focused on the Fourteenth Amendment's equal protection clause. Once he found that legally segregated schooling violated the clause, he had no need to address the issue of due process violations. But in *Bolling v. Sharpe*, the school desegregation case from the District of Columbia that the Court decided along with *Brown*, Warren necessarily reached the due process issue. (Because the Fourteenth Amendment's prohibitive clauses do not apply to the federal government, *Bolling* turned on the due process clause of the Fifth Amendment.) Here, too, Warren declined to reject *Plessy*'s major premise. Rather than flatly holding segregation unreasonable as a matter of law—that is, as inconsistent with the true color-blind character of the amended Constitution, as Harlan had urged in 1896—the Chief Justice in effect admitted that some classifications based on race might be legitimate. Only then did he conclude that "[s]egregation in public education is not reasonably related to any proper governmental objective" and thus violated the due process rights of black school children in the District of Columbia.

Yet *Brown* and its progeny invalidated legislated segregation in a variety of settings and in that sense undeniably struck at the system which *Plessy* had allowed. And if the reasoning in the 1954 opinions showed similarities to the reasoning of 1896, Warren at least did not overtly deny the correctness of Justice Harlan's dissent. In this regard, an argument can be made that if it was legitimate after *Brown* for the Court to rely solely on the 1954 decision as its authority for striking down segregation in non-educational areas, then *Brown* must have turned on the unconstitutionality of *all* racial classification by state agencies. But within a quarter-century, a rather different conclusion was possible.

"Benign" Racial Classification

By the 1970s, attention shifted to affirmative action programs involving preferential or "benign" quotas for members of racial minorities. Their advocates had to show that *Brown* did not mean that *all* racial classifications were per se unconstitutional. In the [*Regents of the University of California v.*] *Bakke* case (1978), the Supreme Court finally faced the issue. It overturned an admissions program of the medical school of the University of California at Davis that set aside sixteen places in each entering class for minority applicants. The Court also held that admissions officers could take account of the racial identity of applicants as one of several non-academic characteristics that might contribute desirable qualities to the overall educational environment. Justice Lewis F. Powell announced the Court's judgment and filed an opinion which gained considerable attention because Powell provided the deciding vote in shaping the Court's two-pronged judgment. He had no good reply to the charge that in some cases such an admissions scheme would in fact use race as the crucial determinant. A court, he could only say, must not presume that university officials would operate the program "as a cover for the functional equivalent of a quota system."

Justice John Paul Stevens, joined by three other members of the Court, strongly objected to any use of race (and thus voted with Powell to overturn the program at the University of California–Davis and to order Allen Bakke's admission). Because Stevens focused on the arrangement at Davis as a statutory violation of the Civil Rights Act of 1964, he avoided extensive constitutional analysis. But lurking only slightly beneath the surface of his opinion was the charge that the Court had rejected Justice Harlan's color-blind Constitution.

Four Justices Reject "Color-Blind" Constitution

What gave real substance to the charge was not Stevens's passing comments, but rather the position taken by the four justices who joined Powell in agreeing that the medical school might still take *some* account of race. These four, who would have preferred to go further and forthrightly accept the university's quota system, spoke out against letting "color blindness become myopia which masks the reality that many [of those] 'created equal' have been treated within our lifetimes as inferior both by the law and by their fellow citizens." Regarding a "color-blind" interpretation of the equal protection clause, they stressed that the Court had "expressly rejected this proposition on a number of occasions."

One of the four, Justice Thurgood Marshall, bore in deeper in a separate opinion. From his review of the events surrounding the adoption of the Fourteenth Amendment, he found it "inconceivable that the . . . Amendment was intended to prohibit all race-conscious relief measures." Reminding his brethren "that the principle that 'the Constitution is color-blind' appeared only in the opinion of the lone dissenter [in *Plessy*]," he left the clear implication that the Constitution should not now be regarded as color-blind. As if to underscore the chasm between his analysis and the one advanced in the 1890s by [Plessy's attorney] Albion Tourgée and Justice Harlan, Marshall portrayed the Declaration of Independence itself as the founding statement of a racist nation. Against this backdrop, racial classification was a requisite to remedying social ills.

The debate over the relation of affirmative action to *Plessy* did not stop with the Court. In the course of defending preferential treatment of minorities, one scholar went so far as to label Harlan's view "color-blind racism" and cautioned, "The courage of Harlan's dissent should not blind us to the moral and historical limitations of his argument." It was a position calculated to ensure white supremacy under the facade of equal protection. Another academician argued that Harlan's slogan about a color-blind Constitution really meant the Constitution was highly sensitive to color. From the other side, a critic of affirmative action charged that the very reasoning used to support supposedly benign racial classifications can be used to support the outcome in *Plessy*, and that Justice Brown's 1896 opinion indeed anticipated the reasoning on behalf of such classifications. After all, Brown had written that "every exercise of the police power must be reasonable, and extend only to such laws as are enacted in good faith for the promotion for the public good, *and not for the annoyance or oppression* of a particular class." Preferential racial classifications were [as author John C. Livingstone wrote in *Fair Game? Inequality and Affirmative Action*] "*Plessy v. Ferguson* all over again, in new and modish dress."

CHAPTER 2

Outlawing School Segregation

Chapter Preface

Case Overview: *Brown v. Board of Education* (1954)

The Supreme Court's decision in *Plessy v. Ferguson* (1896) formalized the doctrine of "separate but equal," meaning that public establishments and private businesses could legally establish separate facilities for whites and blacks as long as the facilities were equal in quality. While separate facilities were common in the South, the "blacks only" facilities were rarely equal to those reserved for whites. Segregation was in effect throughout all areas of life, but the issue of segregating black schoolchildren—in schools that were invariably inferior in quality to white schools—was most hurtful.

Beginning in the 1930s the National Association for the Advancement of Colored People (NAACP) began to target segregation in education. At first the association tried a strategy of ensuring that blacks had truly equal schools. At the same time, black leaders were convinced that segregation itself had to be overturned. They concluded that the very fact of forcing black children to attend separate schools created the inequality that oppressed them.

A series of rulings before 1950 eroded some aspects of segregation but stopped short of overturning the "separate but equal" doctrine. In 1953 the Supreme Court agreed to hear a case brought by African American parents in Topeka, Kansas, challenging segregation in that city. Combined with three other cases filed in Delaware, South Carolina, and Virginia, which all dealt with similar issues, this case would be the final attack on segregation.

The Supreme Court's decision in *Brown v. Board of Education* (1954) was sweeping, completely overturning the *Plessy* doctrine. The Court held that education was essential for participation in American life, both in terms of economic opportunity and good citizenship. As such, public education was the most important aspect of state government. By deliberately segregating a minority, the state stigmatized members of that minority and cut them off from the life of the nation. Thus, despite efforts to make segregated schools equal in faculty, curriculum, and physical facilities, segregation was "inherently unequal," and it was therefore unconstitutional under the equal protection clause of the Fourteenth Amendment.

The contemporary reaction to the *Brown* decision was largely negative. In the South, leaders vowed massive resistance to efforts to integrate schools. Some local school boards went so far as to shut down their entire school systems to prevent black and white children from attending school together. Southern congressmen drafted and signed a document called the "Southern Manifesto," which accused the Supreme Court of acting out of its own "naked power" and disregarding law, tradition, and constitutional principles. Even in the North the decision was criticized, with an editorial in the *New York Times* claiming the Court had not followed constitutional law but had acted on dubious evidence from sociology.

With time, however, *Brown* became accepted and even revered. Today it would be unthinkable for most politicians, commentators, or scholars to criticize the decision. There is criticism, however, of the lack of educational equality between blacks and whites today. Some commentators hold that not enough was done to implement *Brown* and truly integrate schools. Others contend that perhaps the concentration on integration took resources from the more important goal of providing a good education for black children.

Whatever opinion one holds on the ultimate outcome of the case, there is no doubt that *Brown* truly changed America. The legal caste system that relegated blacks to separate facilities and educational institutions has been officially abolished. Although the goal of complete equality has not been achieved, and racial divisions persist in America, *Brown* represents a large step toward the creation of a just and inclusive society.

> *"On numerous occasions the Supreme Court has been asked to overrule the* Plessy *case. This the Supreme Court has refused to do."*

The District Court's Opinion: School Segregation Is Constitutional

Walter Huxman

In 1951 several black families sued in the District Court for the District of Kansas seeking to overturn school segregation laws in the city of Topeka. The school board of Topeka, following the General Statutes of Kansas, had established separate elementary schools for the black and white children of the city. Black children were forced to travel to attend school rather than attending the schools in their own neighborhoods.

The plaintiffs in the lawsuit (the black families) alleged that the black schools' facilities and instruction were not equal to those of the white schools. However, their main complaint was that segregation itself violated black children's right to "due process under the law" as guaranteed in the Fourteenth Amendment to the Constitution. This amendment, passed in the aftermath of the Civil War, was intended to ensure that newly freed blacks and their descendants would enjoy the rights and protections of American citizens.

However, the Supreme Court had ruled in Plessy v. Ferguson *(1896) that "separate but equal" facilities did not violate the equal protection clause of the Fourteenth Amendment. This*

Walter Huxman, opinion, *Brown v. Board of Education*, U.S. District Court of Kansas, 1951.

meant that states could legally segregate blacks in transportation, education, and other public facilities. In this case, the district court upheld Plessy, *ruling that as a subordinate court it could not overturn a Supreme Court precedent. The district court's ruling set up the final stage in this case, a review of the doctrine of "separate but equal" by the Supreme Court in* Brown v. Board of Education.

Chapter 72-1724 of the General Statutes of Kansas, 1949, relating to public schools in cities of the first class, so far as material, authorizes such cities to organize and maintain separate schools for the education of white and colored children in the grades below the high school grades. Pursuant to this authority, the City of Topeka, Kansas, a city of the first class, has established and maintains a segregated system of schools for the first six grades. It has established and maintains in the Topeka School District eighteen schools for white students and four schools for colored students.

The adult plaintiffs instituted this action for themselves, their minor children plaintiffs, and all other persons similarly situated for an interlocutory injunction, a permanent injunction, restraining the enforcement, operation and execution of the state statute and the segregation instituted thereunder by the school authorities of the City of Topeka and for a declaratory judgment declaring unconstitutional the state statute and the segregation set up thereunder by the school authorities of the City of Topeka.

As against the school district of Topeka they contend that the opportunities provided for the infant plaintiffs in the separate all-Negro schools are inferior to those provided white children in the all-white schools; that the respects in which these opportunities are inferior include the physical facilities, curricula, teaching resources, student personnel services as well as all other services. As against both the state and the school district, they contend that apart from all other factors segregation in itself constitutes an inferiority in educational opportunities offered to Negroes and that all of this is in violation of due process guaranteed them by the Fourteenth Amendment to the United States Constitution. In their answer both the state and the school district defends the segregation in its schools instituted thereunder.

School Facilities in Topeka Are Comparable

We have found as a fact that the physical facilities, the curricula, courses of study, qualification of and quality of teachers, as well as other educational facilities in the two sets of schools are comparable. It is obvious that absolute equality of physical facilities is impossible of attainment in buildings that are erected at different times. So also absolute equality of subjects taught is impossible of maintenance where teachers are permitted to select books of their own choosing to use in teaching in addition to the prescribed courses of study. It is without dispute that the prescribed courses of study are identical in all of the Topeka schools and that there is no discrimination in this respect. It is also clear in the record that the educational qualifications of the teachers in the colored schools are equal to those in the white schools and that in all other respects the educational facilities and services are comparable. It is obvious from the fact that there are only four colored schools as against eighteen white schools in the Topeka School District, that colored children in many instances are required to travel much greater distances than they would be required to travel could they attend a white school, and are required to travel much greater distances than white children are required to travel. The evidence, however, establishes that the school district transports colored children to and from school free of charge. No such service is furnished to white children. We conclude that in the maintenance and operation of the schools there is no willful, intentional or substantial discrimination in the matters referred to above between the colored and white schools. In fact, while plaintiffs' attorneys have not abandoned this contention, they did not give it great emphasis in their presentation before the court. They relied primarily upon the contention that segregation in and of itself without more violates their rights guaranteed by the Fourteenth Amendment.

This contention poses a question not free from difficulty. As a subordinate court in the federal judicial system we seek the answer to this constitutional question in the decision of the Supreme Court when it has spoken on the subject and do not substitute our own views for the declared law by the Supreme Court. The difficult question as always is to analyze the decisions and seek to ascertain the trend as revealed by the later decisions.

There are a great number of cases, both federal and state, that have dealt with the many phases of segregation. Since the question involves a construction and interpretation of the federal Constitution and the pronouncements of the Supreme Court, we will consider only those cases by the Supreme Court with respect to segregation in the schools. In the early case of *Plessy v. Ferguson,* the Supreme Court said, "The object of the amendment was undoubtedly to enforce the absolute equality of the two races before the law, but, in the nature of things, it could not have been intended to abolish distinctions based upon color, or to enforce social, as distinguished from political equality, or a commingling of the two races upon terms unsatisfactory to either. Laws permitting, and even requiring, their separation, in places where they are liable to be brought into contract, do not necessarily imply the inferiority of either race to the other, and have been generally, if not universally, recognized as within the competency of the state legislatures in the exercise of their police power. The most common instance of this is connected with the establishment of separate schools for white and colored children, which has been held to be a valid exercise of the legislative power even by courts of states where the political rights of the colored race have been longest and most earnestly enforced."

Previous Cases Uphold Segregation

It is true as contended by plaintiffs that the *Plessy* case involved transportation and that the above quoted statement relating to schools was not essential to the decision of the question before the court and was therefore somewhat in the nature of dicta.[1] But that the statement is considered more than dicta is evidenced by the treatment accorded it by those seeking to strike down segregation as well as by statements in subsequent decisions of the Supreme Court. On numerous occasions the Supreme Court has been asked to overrule the *Plessy* case. This the Supreme Court has refused to do, on the sole ground that a decision of the question was not necessary to a disposal of the controversy presented. In the late case of *Sweatt v. Painter,* the Supreme Court again refused to review the *Plessy* case. The Court said: "Nor need we reach petitioner's contention that *Plessy v. Ferguson* should be reexamined in the light of contemporary knowledge respecting the purposes of the Fourteenth Amendment and the effects of racial segregation."

Gong Lum v. Rice was a grade school segregation case. It involved the segregation law of Mississippi. Gong Lum was a Chinese child and, because of color, was required to attend the separate schools provided for colored children. The opinion of the court assumes that the educational facilities in the colored schools were adequate and equal to those of the white schools. Thus the court said: "The question here is whether a Chinese citizen of the United States is denied equal protection of the laws when he is classed among the colored races and furnished facilities for education equal to that offered to all, whether white, brown, yellow, or black." In addition to nu-

---

1. Dicta are judges' remarks that are not required to reach a decision. They can be commentary on the case, explanatory remarks, or other types of comments.

merous state decisions on the subject, the Supreme Court in support of its conclusions cited *Plessy v. Ferguson*. The Court also pointed out that the question was the same no matter what the color of the class that was required to attend separate schools. Thus the Court said: "Most of the cases cited arose, it is true, over the establishment of separate schools as between white pupils and black pupils; but we cannot think that the question is any different, or that any different result can be reached, assuming the cases above cited to be rightly decided, where the issue is as between white pupils and the pupils of the yellow races." The court held that the question of segregation was within the discretion of the state in regulating its public schools and did not conflict with the Fourteenth Amendment.

A Trend Away from *Plessy*

It is vigorously argued and not without some basis therefore that the later decisions of the Supreme Court in *McLaurin v. Oklahoma* and *Sweatt v. Painter* show a trend away from the *Plessy* and *Lum* cases. *McLaurin v. Oklahoma* arose under the segregation laws of Oklahoma. McLaurin, a colored student, applied for admission to the University of Oklahoma in order to pursue studies leading to a doctorate degree in education. He was denied admission solely because he was a Negro. After litigation in the courts, which need not be reviewed herein, the legislature amended the statute permitting the admission of colored students to institutions of higher learning attended by white students, but providing that such instruction should be given on a segregated basis; that the instruction be given in separate class rooms or at separate times. In compliance with this statute McLaurin was admitted to the university but was required to sit at a separate desk in the ante room adjoining the class room; to sit at a designated desk on the mezzanine floor of the library and to sit at a designated table and eat at a different time from the other students in the school cafeteria. These restrictions were held to violate his rights under the federal Constitution. The Supreme Court held that such treatment handicapped the student in his pursuit of effective graduate instruction.

In *Sweatt v. Painter*, petitioner, a colored student, filed an application for admission to the University of Texas Law School. His application was rejected solely on the ground that he was a Negro. In its opinion the Supreme Court stressed the educational benefits from commingling with white students. The court concluded by stating: "we cannot conclude that the education offered petitioner (in a separate school) is substantially equal to that which he would receive if admitted to the University of Texas Law School." If segregation within a school as in the *McLaurin* case is a denial of due process, it is difficult to see why segregation in separate schools would not result in the same denial. Or if the denial of the right to commingle with the majority group in higher institutions of learning as in the *Sweatt* case and gain the educational advantages resulting therefrom, is lack of due process, it is difficult to see why such denial would not result in the same lack of due process if practiced in the lower grades.

Plessy Has Not Been Overruled

It must however be remembered that in both of these cases the Supreme Court made it clear that it was confining itself to answering the one specific question, namely: "To what extent does the Equal Protection Clause limit the power of a state to distinguish between students of different races in professional and graduate education in a state university?" and that the Supreme Court refused to review the *Plessy* case because that question was not essential to a decision of the controversy in the case.

We are accordingly of the view that the *Plessy* and *Lum* cases have not been overruled and that they still presently are authority for the maintenance of a segregated school system in the lower grades.

> "We conclude that in the field of pub-
> lic education the doctrine of 'sepa-
> rate but equal' has no place. Sepa-
> rate educational facilities are
> inherently unequal."

The Supreme Court's Opinion: Segregated Schools Are Unconstitutional

Earl Warren

The case known as Brown v. Board of Education *(1954) was actually a compilation of a number of cases involving school segregation. All the cases dealt with similar issues, the main contention being whether it was constitutional for public schools to segregate children on the basis of race. In 1952 and 1953 the Supreme Court of the United States heard arguments regarding these cases.*

In the decision, delivered for a unanimous court by Chief Justice Earl Warren, the Court held that the doctrine of "separate but equal," established in Plessy v. Ferguson *(1896), could not be applied in public education. Education was deemed too important for the nation to allow conditions that might impede students' success due to their race. Moreover, sociological studies had shown that segregation stigmatized the members of the minority group, in this case American blacks. For these reasons, segregation in schools was held to be "inherently unequal." The Court relied heavily on history and social science in reaching its decision, a fact that was severely criticized at the time.*

Earl Warren, opinion, *Brown v. Board of Education,* U.S. Supreme Court, 1954.

Warren was chief justice of the United States from 1953 to 1969. He oversaw several landmark decisions upholding individual liberties and civil rights.

These cases come to us from the States of Kansas, South Carolina, Virginia, and Delaware. They are premised on different facts and different local conditions, but a common legal question justifies their consideration together in this consolidated opinion.

In each of the cases, minors of the Negro race, through their legal representatives, seek the aid of the courts in obtaining admission to the public schools of their community on a nonsegregated basis. In each instance, they had been denied admission to schools attended by white children under laws requiring or permitting segregation according to race. This segregation was alleged to deprive the plaintiffs of the equal protection of the laws under the Fourteenth Amendment. In each of the cases other than the Delaware case, a three-judge federal district court denied relief to the plaintiffs on the so-called "separate but equal" doctrine announced by this Court in *Plessy v. Ferguson.* Under that doctrine, equality of treatment is accorded when the races are provided substantially equal facilities, even though these facilities be separate. In the Delaware case, the Supreme Court of Delaware adhered to that doctrine, but ordered that the plaintiffs be admitted to the white schools because of their superiority to the Negro schools.

The plaintiffs contend that segregated public schools are not "equal" and cannot be made "equal," and that hence they are deprived of the equal protection of the laws. Because of the obvious importance of the question presented, the Court took jurisdiction. Argument was heard in the 1952 Term, and reargument was heard this [1953–54] Term on certain questions propounded by the Court.

Controversy over the
Fourteenth Amendment

Reargument was largely devoted to the circumstances surrounding the adoption of the Fourteenth Amendment in 1868.
It covered exhaustively consideration of the Amendment in
Congress, ratification by the states, then existing practices in
racial segregation, and the views of proponents and opponents of the Amendment. This discussion and our own inves-
tigation convince us that, although these sources cast some
light, it is not enough to resolve the problem with which we
are faced. At best, they are inconclusive. The most avid proponents of the post–[Civil] War Amendments undoubtedly intended them to remove all legal distinctions among "all persons born or naturalized in the United States." Their
opponents, just as certainly, were antagonistic to both the letter and the spirit of the Amendments and wished them to
have the most limited effect. What others in Congress and the
state legislatures had in mind cannot be determined with any
degree of certainty.

An additional reason for the inconclusive nature of the
Amendment's history, with respect to segregated schools, is
the status of public education at that time. In the South, the
movement toward free common schools, supported by general
taxation, had not yet taken hold. Education of white children
was largely in the hands of private groups. Education of Negroes was almost nonexistent, and practically all of the race
were illiterate. In fact, any education of Negroes was forbidden by law in some states. Today, in contrast, many Negroes
have achieved outstanding success in the arts and sciences as
well as in the business and professional world. It is true that
public school education at the time of the Amendment had
advanced further in the North, but the effect of the Amendment on Northern States was generally ignored in the congressional debates. Even in the North, the conditions of public

education did not approximate those existing today. The curriculum was usually rudimentary; ungraded schools were common in rural areas; the school term was but three months a year in many states; and compulsory school attendance was virtually unknown. As a consequence, it is not surprising that there should be so little in the history of the Fourteenth Amendment relating to its intended effect on public education.

In the first cases in this Court construing the Fourteenth Amendment, decided shortly after its adoption, the Court interpreted it as proscribing all state-imposed discriminations against the Negro race. The doctrine of "separate but equal" did not make its appearance in this Court until 1896 in the case of *Plessy v. Ferguson,* involving not education but transportation. American courts have since labored with the doctrine for over half a century. In this Court, there have been six cases involving the "separate but equal" doctrine in the field of public education. In *Cumming v. [Richmond] County Board of Education* and *Gong Lum v. Rice,* the validity of the doctrine itself was not challenged. In more recent cases, all on the graduate school level, inequality was found in that specific benefits enjoyed by white students were denied to Negro students of the same educational qualifications. *Missouri ex rel. Gaines v. Canada, Sipuel v. Oklahoma, Sweatt v. Painter, McLaurin v. Oklahoma State Regents.* In none of these cases was it necessary to re-examine the doctrine to grant relief to the Negro plaintiff. And in *Sweatt v. Painter,* the Court expressly reserved decision on the question whether *Plessy v. Ferguson* should be held inapplicable to public education.

In the instant [current] cases, that question is directly presented. Here, unlike *Sweatt v. Painter,* there are findings below that the Negro and white schools involved have been equalized, or are being equalized, with respect to buildings, curricula, qualifications and salaries of teachers, and other "tangible" factors. Our decision, therefore, cannot turn on merely a comparison of these tangible factors in the Negro and white schools involved in each of the cases. We must look instead to the effect of segregation itself on public education.

The Importance of Education

In approaching this problem, we cannot turn the clock back to 1868 when the Amendment was adopted, or even to 1896 when *Plessy v. Ferguson* was written. We must consider public education in the light of its full development and its present place in American life throughout the Nation. Only in this way can it be determined if segregation in public schools deprives these plaintiffs of the equal protection of the laws.

Today, education is perhaps the most important function of state and local governments. Compulsory school attendance laws and the great expenditures for education both demonstrate our recognition of the importance of education to our democratic society. It is required in the performance of our most basic public responsibilities, even service in the armed forces. It is the very foundation of good citizenship. Today it is a principal instrument in awakening the child to cultural values, in preparing him for later professional training, and in helping him to adjust normally to his environment. In these days, it is doubtful that any child may reasonably be expected to succeed in life if he is denied the opportunity of an education. Such an opportunity, where the state has undertaken to provide it, is a right which must be made available to all on equal terms.

Segregation Deprives of Children Equal Opportunity

We come then to the question presented: Does segregation of children in public schools solely on the basis of race, even though the physical facilities and other "tangible" factors may be equal, deprive the children of the minority group of equal educational opportunities? We believe that it does.

In *Sweatt v. Painter,* in finding that a segregated law school for Negroes could not provide them equal educational opportunities, this Court relied in large part on "those qualities which are incapable of objective measurement but which make for greatness in a law school." In *McLaurin v. Oklahoma State Regents,* the Court, in requiring that a Negro admitted to a white graduate school be treated like all other students, again resorted to intangible considerations: ". . . his ability to study, to engage in discussions and exchange views with other students, and, in general, to learn his profession." Such considerations apply with added force to children in grade and high schools. To separate them from others of similar age and qualifications solely because of their race generates a feeling of inferiority as to their status in the community that may affect their hearts and minds in a way unlikely ever to be undone. The effect of this separation on their educational opportunities was well stated by a finding in the Kansas case by a court which nevertheless felt compelled to rule against the Negro plaintiffs:

> Segregation of white and colored children in public schools has a detrimental effect upon the colored children. The impact is greater when it has the sanction of the law; for the policy of separating the races is usually interpreted as denoting the inferiority of the negro group. A sense of inferiority affects the motivation of a child to learn. Segregation with the sanction of law, therefore, has a tendency to [retard] the educational and mental development of negro children and to deprive them of some of the benefits they would receive in a racial[ly] integrated school system.

Whatever may have been the extent of psychological knowledge at the time of *Plessy v. Ferguson,* this finding is amply supported by modern authority. Any language in *Plessy v. Ferguson* contrary to this finding is rejected.

We conclude that in the field of public education the doctrine of "separate but equal" has no place. Separate educational facilities are inherently unequal. Therefore, we hold that the plaintiffs and others similarly situated for whom the actions have been brought are, by reason of the segregation complained of, deprived of the equal protection of the laws guaranteed by the Fourteenth Amendment. This disposition makes unnecessary any discussion whether such segregation also violates the Due Process Clause of the Fourteenth Amendment.

Because these are class actions, because of the wide applicability of this decision, and because of the great variety of local conditions, the formulation of decrees in these cases presents problems of considerable complexity. On reargument the consideration of appropriate relief was necessarily subordinated to the primary question—the constitutionality of segregation in public education. We have now announced that such segregation is a denial of the equal protection of the laws.

> "The Supreme Court ... undertook to exercise their naked judicial power and substituted their personal political and social ideas for the established law of the land."

Brown Violates States' Rights

A Group of Congressmen

Many congressmen from the southern states were outraged by the Brown v. Board of Education *decision in 1954. In response to the ruling, as well as to rising violence in the South in its wake, they composed the "Southern Manifesto." The first draft of the manifesto was written by Strom Thurmond, a long-serving senator. An ardent segregationist, Thurmond downplayed the issue of segregation itself. Rather, he stressed the antidemocratic nature of the Supreme Court's decision.*

The manifesto outlined the history of school segregation, noting that the first segregation law was passed in Massachusetts and that many northern states segregated schools in the early part of the century. Northern segregation was overturned by laws passed through the democratic institutions of the various states. Thurmond and the cosigners of the "Southern Manifesto" held that the voters of each state should have the right to decide whether to maintain segregation. Most controversially, the manifesto praised the efforts of states and local school boards to obstruct the desegregation of schools.

Thurmond's draft was eventually signed by one hundred congressmen from the South (nineteen senators and eighty-one representatives, including almost every congressman from the

Walter F. George et al., "The Southern Manifesto," *Congressional Record,* vol. 102, March 12, 1956.

Deep South). The text of the manifesto was read into the Congressional Record by Walter F. George, a seven-term senator from Georgia.

M r. [Walter F.] GEORGE: Mr. President [of the Senate], the increasing gravity of the situation following the decision of the Supreme Court in the so-called segregation cases, and the peculiar stress in sections of the country where this decision has created many difficulties, unknown and unappreciated, perhaps, by many people residing in other parts of the country, have led some Senators and some Members of the House of Representatives to prepare a statement of the position which they have felt and now feel to be imperative.

I now wish to present to the Senate a statement on behalf of 19 Senators, representing 11 States, and 77 House Members, representing a considerable number of States likewise. . . .

Declaration of Constitutional Principles

The unwarranted decision of the Supreme Court in the public school cases is now bearing the fruit always produced when men substitute naked power for established law.

The Founding Fathers gave us a Constitution of checks and balances because they realized the inescapable lesson of history that no man or group of men can be safely entrusted with unlimited power. They framed this Constitution with its provisions for change by amendment in order to secure the fundamentals of government against the dangers of temporary popular passion or the personal predilections of public officeholders.

We regard the decisions of the Supreme Court in the school cases as a clear abuse of judicial power. It climaxes a trend in the Federal Judiciary undertaking to legislate, in derogation of the authority of Congress, and to encroach upon the reserved rights of the States and the people.

The original Constitution does not mention education. Neither does the 14th Amendment nor any other amendment.

The debates preceding the submission of the 14th Amendment clearly show that there was no intent that it should affect the system of education maintained by the States.

The very Congress which proposed the amendment subsequently provided for segregated schools in the District of Columbia.

When the amendment was adopted in 1868, there were 37 States of the Union. . . .

Segregation Long Approved by Courts

Every one of the 26 States that had any substantial racial differences among its people, either approved the operation of segregated schools already in existence or subsequently established such schools by action of the same law-making body which considered the 14th Amendment.

As admitted by the Supreme Court in the public school case (*Brown v. Board of Education*), the doctrine of separate but equal schools "apparently originated in *Roberts v. City of Boston* (1849), upholding school segregation against attack as being violative of a State constitutional guarantee of equality." This constitutional doctrine began in the North, not in the South, and it was followed not only in Massachusetts, but in Connecticut, New York, Illinois, Indiana, Michigan, Minnesota, New Jersey, Ohio, Pennsylvania and other northern states until they, exercising their rights as states through the constitutional processes of local self-government, changed their school systems.

In the case of *Plessy v. Ferguson* in 1896 the Supreme Court expressly declared that under the 14th Amendment no person was denied any of his rights if the States provided separate but equal facilities. This decision has been followed in many other cases. It is notable that the Supreme Court, speaking through Chief Justice [William H.] Taft, a former President of the United States, unanimously declared in 1927 in *Lum v. Rice* that the "separate but equal" principle is "within the discretion of the State in regulating its public schools and does not conflict with the 14th Amendment."

This interpretation, restated time and again, became a part of the life of the people of many of the States and confirmed their habits, traditions, and way of life. It is founded on elemental humanity and common sense, for parents should not be deprived by Government of the right to direct the lives and education of their own children.

Naked Power of the Courts

Though there has been no constitutional amendment or act of Congress changing this established legal principle almost a century old, the Supreme Court of the United States, with no legal basis for such action, undertook to exercise their naked judicial power and substituted their personal political and social ideas for the established law of the land.

This unwarranted exercise of power by the Court, contrary to the Constitution, is creating chaos and confusion in the States principally affected. It is destroying the amicable relations between the white and Negro races that have been created through 90 years of patient effort by the good people of both races. It has planted hatred and suspicion where there has been heretofore friendship and understanding.

Without regard to the consent of the governed, outside mediators are threatening immediate and revolutionary changes in our public schools systems. If done, this is certain to destroy the system of public education in some of the States.

A Pledge to Oppose Integration

With the gravest concern for the explosive and dangerous condition created by this decision and inflamed by outside meddlers:

We reaffirm our reliance on the Constitution as the fundamental law of the land.

We decry the Supreme Court's encroachment on the rights reserved to the States and to the people, contrary to established law, and to the Constitution.

We commend the motives of those States which have declared the intention to resist forced integration by any lawful means.

We appeal to the States and people who are not directly affected by these decisions to consider the constitutional principles involved against the time when they too, on issues vital to them may be the victims of judicial encroachment.

Even though we constitute a minority in the present Congress, we have full faith that a majority of the American people believe in the dual system of government which has enabled us to achieve our greatness and will in time demand that the reserved rights of the States and of the people be made secure against judicial usurpation.

We pledge ourselves to use all lawful means to bring about a reversal of this decision which is contrary to the Constitution and to prevent the use of force in its implementation.

In this trying period, as we all seek to right this wrong, we appeal to our people not to be provoked by the agitators and troublemakers invading our States and to scrupulously refrain from disorder and lawless acts.

> *"The Court fails to see in these cases
> the opportunity to lay bare the sim-
> plistic hypocrisy of the 'separate but
> equal' standard, not by overturning
> Plessy, but by ordering its strict en-
> forcement."*

Equality in Education Is More Important than Integration

Derrick A. Bell

Derrick A. Bell is a visiting professor of law at New York University and the author of Race, Racism and American Law. *In a chapter written for the book* What Brown v. Board of Education Should Have Said, *in which various legal experts write as if they were justices delivering actual opinions on the* Brown v. Board of Education *case, Bell offers a dissenting opinion. He contends that the Supreme Court in* Brown *has failed to adequately correct the legacy of racism in American society. That racism, legitimized by the 1896* Plessy v. Ferguson *decision legalizing segregation, has allowed whites, both poor and rich, to enjoy privileges that are denied to blacks. Rather than trying to overcome this deep-rooted history by integrating schools, Bell recommends that courts should concentrate on enforcing genuine equality in education by requiring schools to conform to uniform standards. He also calls for minority representation on school boards and in legislative bodies. Bell concludes that these measures will promote equality more effectively than integration, which he predicts will be met with widespread resistance.*

I dissent today from the majority's decision in these cases [that constitute *Brown v. Board of Education*] because the detestable segregation in the public schools that the majority finds unconstitutional is a manifestation of the evil of racism the depths and pervasiveness of which this Court fails even to acknowledge, much less address and attempt to correct.

For reasons that I will explain in some detail, I cannot join in a decision that, while serving well the nation's foreign policy and domestic concerns, provides petitioners with no more than a semblance of the racial equality that they and theirs have sought for so long. The Court's long-overdue findings that Negroes are harmed by racial segregation is, regrettably, unaccompanied by an understanding of the economic, political, and psychological advantages whites gain because of that harm.

With some difficulty, the Court finds that *Plessy v. Ferguson* (1896) cannot now serve as constitutional justification for segregated schools. *Plessy*, though, is only fortuitously a legal precedent. In actuality, it is a judicial affirmation of an unwritten but no less clearly understood social compact that, older than the Constitution, was incorporated into that document, and has been continually affirmed. Chief Justice Roger Taney's observation in *Dred Scott v. Sandford* (1857) that Negroes "had no rights that the white man was bound to respect" was excessive even for its time. The essence of the racial compact, however, is that whites, whatever their status, can view themselves as entitled to privileges and priorities over blacks. Indeed, beyond an appropriate pride in ethnic heritage, this racial compact provides the definitive definition of what it means to be white in America.

The Court Should Enforce "Separate but Equal"

Without recognizing and attempting to dismantle this racial compact and in particular the indirect promises made to whites and the surrender of opportunities whites made to gain these racial privileges, today's decision, while viewed as a triumph by Negro petitioners and the class they represent, will be condemned by many whites as a breach of the compact. Their predictable outraged resistance will undermine and eventually negate judicial enforcement efforts, while political support for the Court's decision, like virtually every other racial rights measure adopted basically to serve white interests once those interests have been served, will become irrelevant.

I regret that the Court fails to see in these cases the opportunity to lay bare the simplistic hypocrisy of the "separate but equal" standard, not by overturning *Plessy*, but by ordering its strict enforcement. Respondents' counsel, John W. Davis, a highly respected advocate, urges this Court to uphold "separate but equal" as the constitutionally correct measure of racial status because, as he puts it so elegantly, "somewhere, sometime to every principle comes a moment of repose when it has been so often announced, so confidently relied upon, so long continued, that it passes the limits of judicial discretion and disturbance."

Elegance, though, should not be allowed to trample truth. The "separate" in the "separate but equal" standard has been rigorously enforced. The "equal" has served as a total refutation of equality. Counsel for the Negro children have gone to great lengths to prove what must be obvious to every person who gives the matter even cursory attention: with some notable exceptions, schools provided for Negroes in segregated systems are unequal in facilities—often obscenely so. And yet, until today, this Court has averted its gaze and has rejected challenges to state-run schools that were both segregated and ruinously unequal. See, e.g., *Cumming v. Richmond County Board of Education* (1899), where this Court refused to order compliance with "separate but equal" at the request of black parents complaining that the school board had closed the black high school while continuing to operate one for whites.

Negro Children Need Education, Not Integration

Responding to a series of challenges in recent years, this Court has acknowledged the flouting of the "separate but equal" standard at the graduate school level. Today, it extends those holdings to encompass segregation in literally thousands of school districts. In doing so, the Court speaks eloquently of the damage segregation does to Negro children's hearts and minds, but the equating of constitutional and educational harm without cognizance of the sources of that harm will worsen the plight of black children for decades to come. By its silent assumption that segregation is an obsolete artifact of a bygone age, the Court sets the stage not for compliance, but for levels of defiance that will prove the antithesis of the equal educational opportunity the petitioners seek.

In their determination to strike down state-mandated segregation, the petitioners ignore the admonishment of [black intellectual] W. E. B. DuBois, one of the nation's finest thinkers. "Negro children need neither segregated schools nor mixed schools. What they need is education." The three phases of relief that I will describe below focus attention on what is needed now by the children of both races. It is the only way to avoid a generation or more of strife over an ideal that, while worthwhile, will not achieve the educationally effective education that petitioners' children need and that existing constitutional standards, stripped of their racist understandings, should provide.

The Court has failed to consider three major components of racial segregation that must be addressed in order to provide meaningful relief. They are:

1. Racial segregation furthers societal stability by subordinating Negro Americans, which makes it easier for rich white Americans to dominate poor white Americans.

2. Negro rights are recognized and protected for only so long as they advance the nation's interests.

3. Realistic rather than symbolic relief for segregated schools will require a specific, judicially monitored plan designed primarily to promote educational equity.

I will discuss each of these components in turn:

Racial Segregation Hurts Negroes and Poor Whites

Racial segregation furthers societal stability by subordinating Negro Americans, which makes it easier for rich white Americans to dominate poor white Americans. Segregation grew out of a series of unofficial racial compromises between white elites and poorer whites who demanded laws segregating public facilities to insure official recognition of their superior status over Negroes, with whom, save for color, they shared a similar economic plight. Yale historian C. Vann Woodward reports that after at first resisting these demands, southern leaders in the post-Reconstruction era enacted segregation laws mainly at the insistence of poor whites, who, given their precarious social and economic status, demanded these barriers to retain a sense of racial superiority over blacks. He observes that "[i]t took a lot of ritual and Jim Crow [legalized discrimination] to bolster the creed of white supremacy in the bosom of a white man working for a black man's wages."

Professor Woodward's quote describes more than it explains. Why would whites conflate Jim Crow laws with real economic well-being? The full answer is likely to be complex, but whites' confusion of race and self-interest is not a recent phenomenon. It dates back to early colonial times. Historians of slavery have shown how plantation owners convinced working-class whites to support slavery even though they could never compete with those who could afford slaves. Slaveholders appealed to working-class whites by urging that their shared whiteness compelled the two groups to unite against the threat of slave revolts or escapes. The strategy worked. In their poverty, whites vented their frustrations by hating the slaves rather than their masters, who held both black slave and free white in economic bondage. When slavery ended, the economic disjuncture, camouflaged by racial division, continued unabated. . . .

Racism Is Central to American Society

[American racism] is the dominant interpretive framework for rendering bodies intelligible. That is to say, racism organizes the American garden's very configuration. Jim Crow was not merely an oppressive legal regime; it consolidated the imaginative lens through which Americans would view race going forward in the future. Jim Crow reaffirmed the binary system through which we (Americans) tend to think of race—i.e., "black" and "white." Jim Crow unceremoniously erased intermediate categories through the biologically ridiculous but politically necessary notion that "one drop" of black blood rendered an individual black. America has not recognized "mulatto," certainly not since post-Reconstruction. The "one drop" concept highlights the rigidity of American racism, and, by virtue of the conceptual currency it continues to enjoy, it makes clear the extent to which Jim Crow segregation was not just a "bad weed." When racism is positioned as a thinking problem (rather than just a "bad weed"), the Court majority's pronouncement can be seen as more a racial provocation than a remedy.

Rather than a now obsolete obstacle to racial equality in the public schools, *Plessy* functioned as a confirmation of myriad racist compromises. Reconstruction precipitated the vastest expansion of federal power since the nation's inception, an expansion for which there would be no match until the New Deal. *Plessy* functioned as a final announcement (to the extent that it was not already clear when Union troops were withdrawn from the South under the terms of the Hayes-Tilden compromise) that the federal government had abdicated any role in restraining state-sponsored racism. As such, the decision normalized post-Reconstruction's racist retrenchment and, concomitantly, the rigid binary structure that racist retrenchment inaugurated. The majority's decision in the present case, of course, does not even begin to address these dimensions of *Plessy*.

By again confirming the historic status of Negroes as the hated and despised "other," *Plessy* marked a transformation in the politics of otherness: the genesis of a new imperative to rigidly fix black people as black. This renewed politics of otherness not only allowed entire categories of poor whites to develop a powerful sense of racial belonging, but allowed entire categories of erstwhile nonwhite immigrants (the Irish are the most prominent example) to become white. The vociferous articulation of rigidly expansive notions of blackness created an entire range of racial opportunities for "would-be" whites.

Petitioners, viewing integration with whites as the only means of overthrowing "separate but equal," urge an end to state-mandated racial segregation. Whites, of course, resist any change in the "separate but equal" standard they view as a vested property right. Resistance under these circumstances is a manifestation of white victimization, willing, it is true, but victimization nevertheless. The question for this Court then is not the obvious one of whether racially segregated schools violate the Equal Protection Clause of the Fourteenth Amendment, but how can this Court grant racial relief desired by Negroes, resisted by whites, and needed by both? As important, how can the relief granted break out of the reform-retrenchment mold that has doomed earlier racial reforms?

Blacks' Rights and the National Interest

Negro rights are recognized and protected for only so long as they advance the nation's interests. This Court's decision will replicate a familiar pattern of relief for racial injustices. A semblance of justice for Negroes serves as the vehicle for furthering interests of the nation. Examining the history of civil rights policies, we find that even the most serious injustices suffered by Negroes, including slavery, segregation, and patterns of murderous violence, are not sufficient to gain real relief from any branch of government. Rather, relief from racial discrimination, when it comes, requires that policy makers perceive that the relief will provide a clear benefit for the nation. While it is nowhere mentioned in the majority's opinion, it is quite clear that a major motivation for the Court to outlaw racial segregation now when it declined to do so in the past is the major boost this decision will provide in our competition with communist governments abroad and our fight to uproot subversive elements at home.

It is likely that not since the Civil War has the need to remedy racial injustice been so firmly aligned with the country's vital interests at home and abroad. The majority's ringing statement will provide a symbolic victory to petitioners and the class of Negroes they represent while, in fact, giving a new, improved face to the nation's foreign policy and responding to charges of blatant racial bias at home, thus furnishing a fresh example of the historic attraction to granting recognition and promising reform of racial injustice when such action converges with the nation's interests.

I do not ignore the potential value of this Court's simply recognizing the evil of segregation, an evil Negroes have experienced first-hand for too long. There is, I also agree, a place for symbols in law for a people abandoned by law for much of the nation's history. I recognize and hail the impressive manner in which Negroes have made symbolic gains and given them meaning by the sheer force of their belief. Is it not precisely because of their unstinting faith in this country's ideals that they deserve better than an expression of benign paternalism, no matter how well intended? It will serve as a sad substitute for the needed empathy of action called for when a history of racial subordination is to be undone.

The racial reform-retrenchment pattern so evident here indicates that when the tides of white resentment rise and again swamp the expectations of Negroes in a flood of racial hostility, this Court and likely the country will vacillate. Then, as with the Emancipation Proclamation and the Civil War Amendments, it will rationalize its inability and—let us be honest—its unwillingness to give real meaning to the rights we declare so readily and so willingly sacrifice when our interests turn to new issues, more pressing concerns.

Judges Need to Promote Educational Equality

Realistic rather than symbolic relief for segregated schools will require a specific, judicially monitored plan designed primarily to promote educational equity. While declaring racial segregation harmful to black children, the majority treats these policies as though they descended unwanted from the skies and can now be mopped up like a heavy rainfall and flushed away. The fact is that, as my brief review of the nation's racial history makes clear, a great many white as well as Negro children have been harmed by segregation. Segregation requires school systems to operate duplicate sets of schools that are as educationally inefficient as their gross incompliance with the "separate but equal" *Plessy* mandate makes them constitutionally deficient.

Pressured by this litigation, the school boards assure this Court that they are taking steps to equalize facilities in Negro schools. More important than striking down *Plessy v. Ferguson* is the need to reveal its hypocritical underpinnings by requiring its full enforcement for all children, white as well as black. Full enforcement requires more than either equalizing facilities or, in the case of Delaware because of the inadequacy of the Negro schools, ordering plaintiffs admitted into the white schools. As a primary step toward the disestablishment of the dual school system, I would order relief that must be provided all children in racially segregated districts in three phases:

Phase 1: Equalization. (1) Effective immediately on receipt of this Court's mandate, school officials of the respondent school districts must ascertain through appropriate measures the academic standing of each school district as compared with nationwide norms for school systems of comparable size and financial resources. This data will be published and made available to all patrons of the district. (2) All schools within the district must be fully equalized in physical facilities, teacher training, experience, and salary with the goal that each district as a whole will measure up to national norms within three years.

Phase 2. Representation. The battle cry of those who fought and died to bring this country into existence was "Taxation without representation is tyranny." Effective relief in segregated school districts requires no less than the immediate restructuring of school boards and other policy-making bodies to insure that those formally excluded from representation have persons selected by them in accordance with the percentage of their children in the school system. This restructuring must take effect no later than the start of the 1955–56 school year.

Phase 3. Judicial oversight. To implement these orders efficiently, federal district judges should be instructed to set up three-person monitoring committees, with the Negro and white communities each selecting a monitor and those two agreeing on a third. The monitoring committees will work with school officials to prepare the necessary plans and procedures enabling the school districts to comply with phases 1 and 2. The district courts will oversee compliance and will address firmly any actions intended to subvert or hinder the compliance program.

In my view, the petitioners' goal—the disestablishment of the dual school system—will be more effectively achieved for students, parents, teachers, administrators, and other individuals connected directly or indirectly with the school system by these means than by the majority's ringing order, which I fear will not be effectively enforced and will be vigorously resisted.

> "Chief Justice Earl Warren's unani-
> mous opinion . . . was every bit as
> important a document as the Dec-
> laration of Independence or the
> Constitution."

Brown Was a Landmark for Civil Rights

Edward Lazarus

*Edward Lazarus practices and teaches law in Los Angeles. He is
a columnist for the Internet site FindLaw and has written two
books about the Supreme Court.*

In this selection Lazarus defends the Brown v. Board of
Education *opinion as one of the most important documents in
American history. He notes that many blacks, particular older
ones, divide history into pre-*Brown *and post-*Brown *eras. Pre-*
Brown *African Americans were subject to humiliation and oppression, Lazarus points out, while the post-*Brown *era has been
a time of opportunity. While the* Brown *decision has not transformed American society totally, he argues, it has given America
a yardstick against which to measure its commitment to freedom
and justice.*

Not long ago, I heard a speech by a leading black civil
rights figure from the 1960s and 70s about *Brown v.
Board of Education,* a decision that celebrates its 50th birthday
[in 2004]. To this son of the Jim Crow South, Chief Justice
Earl Warren's unanimous opinion—famously repudiating the

Edward Lazarus, "Evaluating *Brown v. Board of Education* on Its Fiftieth Anniversary:
Are the Revisionists Right About This Landmark Decision?" *FindLaw,* April 29, 2004.
Copyright © 2004 by *FindLaw,* a Thomson business. This column originally appeared
on FindLaw.com. Reproduced by permission.

doctrine of "separate but equal," and ending legalized segregation in public schools—was every bit as important a document as the Declaration of Independence or the Constitution.

This was not hyperbole on his part. Looking back from his current vantagepoint as a corporate titan, this man described *Brown* as essential not just to his success, but to the very creation of his ambition. Quite simply, his life divided into two parts, pre-*Brown* and post-*Brown*—one marked by humiliation and oppression, the other by possibilities and dreams.

What struck me about this speech was not so much its content, as its familiarity. I have heard many blacks of this man's generation speak about *Brown*. Their basic message has always been the same: *Brown* changed everything for blacks, as nothing had before or has since.

This message is out of fashion now. It's true that *Brown*'s anniversary will spawn dozens of conferences, articles and books devoted to the case. And it's true that the "rightness" of *Brown* is now publicly unassailable. Nevertheless, the revisionists have taken hold of the decision's legacy and tell us with ever-greater certainty that its true import is much more modest than one might imagine.

Are the revisionists correct? In this column I will examine why they might, or might not, be.

The Reasons for the Revisionism About *Brown*

Both history and current social reality provide plenty of grist for the revisionist mill.

Southern resistance to *Brown* (abetted by President Dwight Eisenhower's negative reaction, and the Supreme Court's own decision to order desegregation to occur "with all deliberate speed," in *Brown II*,[1] rather than to occur immediately) effectively delayed *Brown*'s meaningful implementation. As a matter of fact, as opposed to law, public schools in the South remained almost totally segregated for more than a decade.

Worse still, public attitudes and the Supreme Court itself have significantly undermined the eventual progress that was made toward public school integration. The combination of "white flight" to the suburbs, and the Supreme Court's refusal to permit inter-district busing, have turned many inner-city schools into nearly all-black ghettos of inferior resources and education.

In light of this sad reality, revisionists ask whether *Brown*, as a practical matter, has accomplished very much at all.

Revisionists also point out that *Brown* had little practical impact outside the field of education. After 1954, hotels and restaurants and buses across the South remained segregated. Many states continued to outlaw interracial marriage (until the Supreme Court's decision in *Loving v. Virginia*), and imposed nearly insurmountable obstacles to black voter registration. Discrimination in almost every form remained a standard part of life across large swaths of America.

Racial bigotry, at least in its overt manifestations, did not recede because of *Brown*, these revisionists tell us. Instead, real progress occurred only after Congress stepped in and passed the landmark civil rights legislation of the mid- and late 1960s, outlawing a host of both public and private acts of race discrimination.

The Reasons We Should Not Embrace Revisionism

No doubt all this is true. But it is also, to my mind, largely beside the point.

1. In *Brown II*, the Supreme Court decided on the means that local school boards should use to desegregate their schools. The Court allowed the school boards to desegregate slowly, as the phrase "with all deliberate speed" signifies.

As an initial matter, I have never thought that *Brown* was really about segregation in public schools, except in the most literal sense. *Brown* was about putting an end to state-sponsored and state-approved racial oppression.

In this respect, *Brown* cannot be thought of in isolation. At a minimum, it must be coupled with the many other decisions of the Warren Court that embodied the spirit and principles of *Brown.*

What was the gist of all these decisions, taken together? Simply put, it was to demand—and to order—the end of four centuries of racial degradation. It was also to declare that, at least under law, the state may not humiliate blacks by setting them apart or punishing them for sharing the aspirations of their fellow citizens.

Such decisions include, most obviously, *Cooper v. Aaron,* in which the justices, again unanimously, stood fast during the Little Rock school crisis when Arkansas Governor Orval Faubus defied *Brown's* mandate. It took federal troops to dislodge Faubus from the schoolhouse door, but in the end, the Court, and the rule of law, prevailed.

Beyond the issue of education, the justices worked to open up the political process for blacks by forcing the redrawing of electoral districts according to the principle of one-person/one-vote. Thanks to that decision (*Baker v. Carr*), blacks slowly started winning public office in the South.

The Court also tried to protect blacks against the worst abuses of state officials by giving them ever-wider access to federal courts to vindicate their rights. And, perhaps even more important, the justices vested Congress with ever greater authority to outlaw race discrimination in public and private life.

All this, it seems to me, must be deemed a part of *Brown's* legacy—and that is monumental, even if in these fields, as in our public schools, the achievements on the ground have been halting and imperfect.

Brown's Legacy Remains Invaluable

Even more important, *Brown*'s legacy is not properly discounted (as some seem to [believe]) because the decision did not achieve a magical transformation of law or society. This is far beyond the power of any single judicial decision, or even collection of decisions.

Ultimately, the effectiveness of the Supreme Court's work is hostage to the commitment of the President and Congress and, most important, to the receptiveness of the American people to [the] legal principles announced. In the case of *Brown*, that commitment has too often been equivocal.

Rather, what makes the legacy of *Brown* so profound— what makes blacks of a certain generation speak of it with such awe and reverence—is its embodiment of an ideal of racial and social justice.

That ideal has eluded every society since the beginning of time. It is a Platonic form to be yearned for, that may never quite be achieved.

But prior to *Brown*, as a matter of national law, there was not even a yearning. *Brown* changed that, forever. It gave Americans a measuring stick for their aspiration to be a country truly just and free—and, better yet, it created a stick that could be seen, and held, and wielded, by a racial group ground down by 400 years of legal subjugation. (Moreover, in arguing the case before the Supreme Court for the NAACP [National Association for the Advancement of Colored People], Thurgood Marshall became an indelible role model for all that for which he argued.)

This is an achievement well worth celebrating, and will be again in another 50 years, and 50 years beyond that, and for as long as we can remember the evil that bigotry is.

"Are we satisfied with our progress,
or have we given up on our ideal of
equality?"

The Effects of *Brown* Are Being Eroded

Phillip Boyle

Phillip Boyle is associate professor of public management and government in the School of Government, University of North Carolina at Chapel Hill. In this essay Boyle recounts how the plaintiffs in the Brown v. Board of Education *case saw their mission as a moral one. When they succeeded in getting legal segregation overturned, many opinion leaders throughout the United States celebrated. However, over time some of the gains of* Brown *have been reversed. Boyle uses a variety of sources to show that schools have become more segregated over the last few decades as parents seek more control over where their children go to school.*

B*rown* is often cited to justify the value of an independent judiciary or to illustrate the importance of constitutional protections for minority rights and often criticized for its presumed lack of judicial neutrality and abuse of judicial authority. But *Brown* is more than a legal decision. It is a statement about the fundamental moral basis of democracy. As Andrew Hacker argues in *Two Nations: Black and White, Separate, Hostile, Unequal* :

> A century and a quarter after slavery, white America contin-
> ues to ask of its black citizens an extra patience and perse-

verance that whites have never required of themselves. So the question for white Americans is essentially moral: is it right to impose on members of an entire race a lesser start in life, and then to expect from them a degree of resolution that has never been demanded from your own race?

The plaintiffs in *Brown* also understood the moral basis of their case—an equal opportunity, already afforded to most other Americans, to realize the American Dream. In his online article "The Supreme Court Decision That Changed a Nation," David Pitts captures this in the words of the plaintiffs. "I'm a very old woman now, but if I had to do it again, I would," says Vivian Scales, one of the Topeka parents. "When you get right down to it, the message of the *Brown* decision and the memorial is really that all human beings of all races are created equal," adds Zelma Henderson, another parent. "We went to the Supreme Court of the United States to affirm that fact, and we won."

Brown Was a Moral Decision

On May 18, 1954, many of the nation's newspapers praised the Court's decision in moral terms. As the *New York Times* wrote on its editorial pages, "The highest court in the land, the guardian of our national conscience, has reaffirmed its faith and the undying American faith in the equality of all men and all children before the law." And the *Washington Post and Times Herald* wrote that the court's decision will ". . . help to refurbish American prestige in a world which looks to this land for moral inspiration and restore the faith of Americans themselves in their own great values and traditions."

The true lesson of *Brown* is that democracy matters, that civic virtues and values matter, and that democracy rests upon a moral foundation. While much has been made of the degree to which the Court relied upon social science research, its decision focused not on science, but on values, ideals, and morality. As Deborah Stone notes in *Policy Paradox,* the *Brown* opinion "relegates social science to a footnote, and gains its persuasive power instead by evoking our compassion for black children."

Good public decisions preserve the fundamental values that underlie every public choice. Just decisions balance these competing values. When we pursue one public value to the exclusion of the others, or when we restrict others from their pursuit of public values, we act unjustly. Such injustice harms not only the individuals and values involved, but also democracy itself. The *Brown* court, consistent with the authors of the Federalist Papers (Alexander Hamilton, John Jay, and James Madison) and with [Alexis de] Tocqueville and Martin Luther King Jr., helped us steer a course for the future by contrasting where we were with where we could be as a democratic society. . . .

Why *Brown* Still Matters Today

In 1938 the Carnegie Corporation commissioned Swedish economist Gunnar Myrdal to study the lives of black Americans. In *An American Dilemma: The Negro Problem and Modern Democracy,* one of the handful of social science works cited by the *Brown* court, Myrdal described Americans as caught in an "ever-raging conflict" between the values of the "American Creed," particularly equality and justice, and the social and economic prejudices of an individualistic and post-slavery society.

One way a democratic society resolves this dilemma is through institutions that amplify these values, such as the church, the school, and the state. As Myrdal writes, "The school, in every community, is likely to be a degree more broadminded than local opinion. So is the sermon in church. . . . Legislation will, on the whole, be more equitable than the legislators are themselves as private individuals."

While institutions reflect passions and prejudices—how could they do otherwise, when they are made up of individuals?—they are nonetheless "devoted to certain broad ideals," Myrdal writes. "It is in these institutions that the American Creed has its instruments: it plays upon them as on mighty organs." We place in these institutions our "ideals of how the world rightly ought to be."

Diversity Versus Personal Freedom

Public schools matter in the quest for equality precisely because they are public and, therefore, repositories for our ideals. Public schools also matter because it is in schools that the tension between equality and individual choice is felt most strongly—and where the impact of *Brown* is being eroded. Consider the following examples, drawn from North Carolina, in which this tension is played out:

The Wake County Public School System, with a long-standing commitment to academic excellence and student diversity, has adopted a policy of student assignment that uses socioeconomic data to ensure that no school in the system has more than 40 percent of its students eligible for free or reduced-price lunches. A group of citizens, including some parents, a local Chamber of Commerce, and some local elected officials, object to this policy. Citing personal freedom, parental rights, safety, and inconvenience, they formed ABC, Assignment By Choice. The members of ABC believe that all parents should be able to choose the school they believe is in the best interests of their children without interference from the school board.

And in the Chapel Hill-Carrboro district, the decision to adopt "differentiation" rather than tracking was the subject of a [Raleigh, N.C.] *News & Observer* column by Rick Martinez, who suggests that the "elusive quest for equality gets in the way of meaningful progress for minorities." Martinez writes that differentiation—meaning that classes contain students of all abilities and socioeconomic backgrounds—sounds great in theory, but in practice it has "a dark side that impedes achievement and limits opportunity."

Tracking, on the other hand, may offer exceptional opportunities for exceptional students, but it does little for all the other students. Clearly, there is no easy answer here or in Wake County.

Reversing *Brown*

Individual opportunity is good for individuals, but equal opportunity is good for everyone. Unfortunately, equal opportunity is becoming less equal. At the peak of desegregation, nearly half of all black students attended predominantly white schools. By the late 1980s this trend had begun to reverse.

Today, 70 percent of black students attend predominantly minority schools, with more than one-third attending schools that are at least 90 percent minority. The figures are similar for Hispanic students. Less than a third of white students go to school with black or Hispanic students. Already, a majority of the students in six states and the District of Columbia are not white.

If the *Brown* decision was about school desegregation, the 50th anniversary of *Brown* is very much about school resegregation. Gary Orfield and his colleagues at Harvard University's Civil Rights Project have concluded that resegregation has become a national trend. In *Dismantling Desegregation: The Quiet Reversal of* Brown v. Board of Education, they describe the set of court cases during the 1980s and 1990s that moved away from *Brown* as "resegregation decisions." And in *Schools More Separate: Consequences of a Decade of Resegregation,* they write, "There is considerable confusion about the status of desegregation law, but the basic trend is toward dissolution of desegregation orders and return to patterns of more serious segregation."

It is not just schools that are experiencing resegregation and new patterns of segregation, though, as shown by recent studies of housing and residential patterns in Boston, Chicago, and San Diego.

Continuing Inequality

Are we satisfied with our progress, or have we given up on our ideal of equality? In the America of 2004, Martin Luther King Jr. has been elevated to the status of national icon, and celebrations of *Brown* will be held across the country. Most Americans want to believe that we have corrected the inequities of the past, that there is no longer any need for collective action and sacrifice on behalf of racial equality. But the facts reveal the chilling distance between the America of King's dream and the American Dream for most black Americans today. In *The Anatomy of Racial Inequality*, Glenn Loury describes how social life in the United States continues to be characterized by significant racial stratification:

> Numerous indices of well-being—wages, unemployment rates, income and wealth levels, ability test scores, prison enrollment and crime victimization rates, health and mortality statistics—all reveal substantial racial disparities. Indeed, over the past quarter-century the disadvantage of blacks along many of these dimensions has remained unchanged, or, in some instances, has even worsened.

Today the United States has the most diverse population of public school students in its history. Because public education will become the first major nonwhite institution, how we treat school segregation will influence the larger American society for generations to come. School segregation will have serious consequences not only for minority students, but also for white students, who will enter a society and its workplaces that are increasingly black and brown.

CHAPTER 3

Declaring Hate Crime Laws Constitutional

Chapter Preface

Case Overview: *Wisconsin v. Mitchell* (1993)

In October 1989 a young white boy named Gregory Riddick was attacked by a group of young black men. The attackers had recently discussed the film *Mississippi Burning,* which depicted anti-black racial violence in the South. Motivated by the film, Todd Mitchell asked the group, "Do you feel all hyped up to move on some white people?" Seeing Riddick on the street, Mitchell reportedly said, "There goes a white boy, go get him." Riddick was beaten by the group so badly he spent four days in a coma.

When Mitchell went to trial for his role in the attack, prosecutors asked for a "sentence enhancement," which under Wisconsin law allows for heavier penalties for crimes committed due to racial, ethnic, or religious hatred. Once Mitchell was convicted, his lawyers appealed the heavier sentence, holding that it was unconstitutional to impose a harsher sentence on a crime based on the motives of the criminal. While racial or ethnic hatred is odious, they argued, under the U.S. Constitution people are free to think odious thoughts. Mitchell certainly could be punished for the crime of instigating the attack on Riddick, but he could not be punished more severely due to his thought, or even speech, before the crime.

The first court of appeals rejected these arguments from Mitchell's attorneys, but the Wisconsin State Supreme Court ruled in favor of Mitchell, expressing concern that imposing extra penalties for motivations could lead to a "chilling" of free speech. The State of Wisconsin then appealed to the U.S. Supreme Court.

The Supreme Court had recently ruled in *R.A.V. v. St. Paul* that speech codes designed to prevent racially or ethnically inflammatory speech were unconstitutional. Because of this precedent it seemed likely that the Court would find sentence enhancement in the Wisconsin law also unconstitutional. However, the Court returned a unanimous decision reversing the Wisconsin State Supreme Court and finding against Mitchell. Imposing harsher penalties due to the motive behind the criminal action was constitutional, ruled the Court.

In a unanimous opinion penned by Chief Justice William Rehnquist, the high court found that acts of violence had never been included among free speech rights guaranteed under the First Amendment. Speech—such as Mitchell's—that was designed to incite violence and was immediately associated with a violent act could not fall under First Amendment rights. Second, there are cases in which government does consider motives when determining the nature of a crime, and thus the final punishment. For example, many of the provisions of the 1964 Civil Rights Act punish people for their intention to discriminate even though specific acts such as denying rental housing are legal if the motive behind a denial is not racial prejudice. In cases of treason the government is required to determine that the accused "adhered to the enemy." In this instance as well the government must determine the motive behind the accused person's action.

Rehnquist distinguished this case from the earlier *R.A.V.* case. In that case the city of St. Paul, Minnesota, had outlawed expressions that were likely to arouse feelings against—or reactions from—ethnic or religious minorities. The St. Paul law did not require that an "underlying crime" be committed. In the Wisconsin statute, a crime was necessary to bring the harsher penalty into effect. It was the crime itself, not the thoughts of the perpetrator, that made the defendant liable for criminal punishment. Once a crime had been proven, however, the state certainly could impose stiffer penalties for motivations it judged to be especially harmful for society.

> "The First Amendment ... does not prohibit the evidentiary use of speech to establish the elements of a crime or to prove motive or intent."

The Court's Opinion: Hate Crime Laws Do Not Violate Free Speech Rights

William H. Rehnquist

William H. Rehnquist was a Supreme Court justice for thirty-three years (from 1972 to 2005), the last nineteen of which he served as chief justice. Rehnquist was known as a conservative; he died in office after a battle with cancer.

The following selection is excerpted from the unanimous opinion written by Rehnquist in the Wisconsin v. Mitchell *case. Rehnquist dismisses the claim that a Wisconsin hate crimes statute violates the First Amendment's guarantee of free speech. The law does not punish speech, he insists, but merely imposes an enhanced punishment for violent crimes motivated by hate. Rehnquist reviews the Court's prior cases and notes that violent action has never been granted free-speech protection. Moreover, courts have long considered motivation both when determining guilt and when sentencing for crimes. Rehnquist concludes that the Constitution's framers intended to allow consideration of motives when determining the severity of punishment for crimes. This means that modern lawmakers can also take motives such as racial or ethnic hatred into account when determining sentences for crimes against persons or property.*

William H. Rehnquist, opinion, *Wisconsin v. Mitchell,* U.S. Supreme Court, 1993.

T he State [of Wisconsin] argues that the [hate crime] statute does not punish bigoted thought, as the Supreme Court of Wisconsin said, but instead punishes only conduct. While this argument is literally correct, it does not dispose of [Todd] Mitchell's First Amendment challenge. To be sure, our cases reject the "view that an apparently limitless variety of conduct can be labeled 'speech' whenever the person engaging in the conduct intends thereby to express an idea." *United States v. O'Brien* (1968). Thus, a physical assault is not, by any stretch of the imagination, expressive conduct protected by the First Amendment.

Wisconsin Statute Punishes Motives

But the fact remains that under the Wisconsin statute the same criminal conduct may be more heavily punished if the victim is selected because of his race or other protected status than if no such motive obtained. Thus, although the statute punishes criminal conduct, it enhances the maximum penalty for conduct motivated by a discriminatory point of view more severely than the same conduct engaged in for some other reason or for no reason at all. Because the only reason for the enhancement is the defendant's discriminatory motive for selecting his victim, *Mitchell* argues (and the Wisconsin Supreme Court held) that the statute violates the First Amendment by punishing offenders' bigoted beliefs.

Traditionally, sentencing judges have considered a wide variety of factors in addition to evidence bearing on guilt in determining what sentence to impose on a convicted defendant. The defendant's motive for committing the offense is one important factor. Thus, in many States, the commission of a murder or other capital offense for pecuniary gain is a separate aggravating circumstance under the capital sentencing statute.

But it is equally true that a defendant's abstract beliefs, however obnoxious to most people, may not be taken into consideration by a sentencing judge. In *Dawson* [*v. Delaware*], the State introduced evidence at a capital sentencing hearing that the defendant was a member of a white supremacist prison gang. Because "the evidence proved nothing more than [the defendant's] abstract beliefs," we held that its admission violated the defendant's First Amendment rights. In so holding, however, we emphasized that "the Constitution does not erect a per se barrier to the admission of evidence concerning one's beliefs and associations at sentencing simply because those beliefs and associations are protected by the First Amendment." Thus, in *Barclay v. Florida* (1983) we allowed the sentencing judge to take into account the defendant's racial animus towards his victim. The evidence in that case showed that the defendant's membership in the Black Liberation Army and desire to provoke a "race war" were related to the murder of a white man for which he was convicted. Because "the elements of racial hatred in [the] murder" were relevant to several aggravating factors, we held that the trial judge permissibly took this evidence into account in sentencing the defendant to death.

Mitchell suggests that *Dawson* and *Barclay* are inapposite [not relevant] because they did not involve application of a penalty-enhancement provision. But in *Barclay* we held that it was permissible for the sentencing court to consider the defendant's racial animus in determining whether he should be sentenced to death, surely the most severe "enhancement" of all. And the fact that the Wisconsin Legislature has decided, as a general matter, that bias-motivated offenses warrant greater maximum penalties across the board does not alter the result here. For the primary responsibility for fixing criminal penalties lies with the legislature.

Bias Crime Laws Similar to Antidiscrimination Laws

Mitchell argues that the Wisconsin penalty-enhancement statute is invalid because it punishes the defendant's discriminatory motive, or reason, for acting. But motive plays the same role under the Wisconsin statute as it does under federal and state antidiscrimination laws, which we have previously upheld against constitutional challenge. Title VII of the Civil Rights Act of 1964, for example, makes it unlawful for an employer to discriminate against an employee "because of such individual's race, color, religion, sex, or national origin." In *Hishon* [*v. King and Spolding*], we rejected the argument that Title VII infringed employers' First Amendment rights. And more recently, in *R.A.V. v. St. Paul,* we cited Title VII as an example of a permissible content-neutral regulation of conduct.

Nothing in our decision last Term in *R. A. V.* compels a different result here. That case involved a First Amendment challenge to a municipal ordinance prohibiting the use of "'fighting words' that insult, or provoke violence, 'on the basis of race, color, creed, religion or gender.'" Because the ordinance only proscribed a class of "fighting words" deemed particularly offensive by the city—i.e., those "that contain . . . messages of 'bias-motivated' hatred," we held that it violated the rule against content-based discrimination. But whereas the ordinance struck down in *R. A. V.* was explicitly directed at expression (i.e., "speech" or "messages"), the statute in this case is aimed at conduct unprotected by the First Amendment.

Moreover, the Wisconsin statute singles out for enhancement bias-inspired conduct because this conduct is thought to inflict greater individual and societal harm. For example, according to the State . . . bias-motivated crimes are more likely to provoke retaliatory crimes, inflict distinct emotional harms on their victims, and incite community unrest. The State's desire to redress these perceived harms provides an adequate explanation for its penalty-enhancement provision over and above mere disagreement with offenders' beliefs or biases. As [eighteenth-century English legal scholar William] Blackstone said long ago, "it is but reasonable that among crimes of different natures, those should be most severely punished, which are the most destructive of the public safety and happiness."

Wisconsin Law Does Not Chill Free Speech

Finally, there remains to be considered *Mitchell*'s argument that the Wisconsin statute is unconstitutionally overbroad because of its "chilling effect" on free speech. *Mitchell* argues (and the Wisconsin Supreme Court agreed) that the statute is "overbroad" because evidence of the defendant's prior speech or associations may be used to prove that the defendant intentionally selected his victim on account of the victim's protected status. Consequently, the argument goes, the statute impermissibly chills free expression with respect to such matters by those concerned about the possibility of enhanced sentences if they should in the future commit a criminal offense covered by the statute. We find no merit in this contention.

The sort of chill envisioned here is far more attenuated and unlikely than that contemplated in traditional "overbreadth" cases. We must conjure up a vision of a Wisconsin citizen suppressing his unpopular bigoted opinions for fear that if he later commits an offense covered by the statute, these opinions will be offered at trial to establish that he selected his victim on account of the victim's protected status, thus qualifying him for penalty enhancement. To stay within the realm of rationality, we must surely put to one side minor misdemeanor offenses covered by the statute, such as negligent operation of a motor vehicle, for it is difficult, if not impossible, to conceive of a situation where such offenses would be racially motivated. We are left, then, with the prospect of a citizen suppressing his bigoted beliefs for fear that evidence of such beliefs will be introduced against him at trial if he commits a more serious offense against person or property. This is simply too speculative a hypothesis to support *Mitchell*'s overbreadth claim.

The First Amendment, moreover, does not prohibit the evidentiary use of speech to establish the elements of a crime or to prove motive or intent. Evidence of a defendant's previous declarations or statements is commonly admitted in criminal trials subject to evidentiary rules dealing with relevancy, reliability, and the like. Nearly half a century ago, in *Haupt v. United States* (1947), we rejected a contention similar to that advanced by *Mitchell* here. Haupt was tried for the offense of treason, which, as defined by the Constitution (Art. III, 3), may depend very much on proof of motive. To prove that the acts in question were committed out of "adherence to the enemy" rather than "parental solicitude," the Government introduced evidence of conversations that had taken place long prior to the indictment, some of which consisted of statements showing Haupt's sympathy with Germany and Hitler and hostility towards the United States. We rejected Haupt's argument that this evidence was improperly admitted. While "[s]uch testimony is to be scrutinized with care to be certain the statements are not expressions of mere lawful and permissible difference of opinion with our own government or quite proper appreciation of the land of birth," we held that "these statements . . . clearly were admissible on the question of intent and adherence to the enemy."

For the foregoing reasons, we hold that Mitchell's First Amendment rights were not violated by the application of the Wisconsin penalty-enhancement provision in sentencing him.

> "Bias-related tensions, particularly those involving race, have consistently sparked this nation's most violent and disruptive civil disorders."

Hate Crimes' Destructiveness Justifies Stricter Sentences

Henry J. Silberberg

Henry J. Silberberg was the counsel of record for a group of organizations that wanted the U.S. Supreme Court to reinstate the Wisconsin hate crime law. At the time of writing of the following amicus curiae brief for Wisconsin v. Mitchell, *he was employed by the law firm Stroock, Stroock and Lavan.*

In his brief Silberberg stresses the special nature of bias crimes (also called hate crimes). He contends that they are random and irrational and that those committing such crimes are likely to be repeat offenders. Moreover, hate crimes are difficult to deter through ordinary legislation and often spark further tensions within a community, leading to a cycle of violence between groups. For all these reasons, states have a legitimate interest in imposing harsher penalties for crimes that target individuals merely because of their membership in a racial, ethnic, religious, or other group.

The Wisconsin Criminal Code provides for enhanced punishment when the State proves that a convicted criminal "[i]ntentionally selects the person against whom the crime . . . is committed because of the race, religion, color, disability,

Henry J. Silberberg et al., amici curiae brief, *Wisconsin v. Mitchell,* U.S. Supreme Court, 1992.

sexual orientation, national origin or ancestry of that person. . . ."

Bias Crime Statutes Are Justified

The Wisconsin Supreme Court incorrectly held that the Wisconsin statute violates the First Amendment because it punishes "what the Legislature has deemed to be offensive thought. . . ." *State of Wisconsin v. Mitchell* (1992). The statute represents a legitimate exercise of the State's police power to protect the health, safety and welfare of its citizens and does not, in any way, impermissibly infringe upon First Amendment rights. . . . Even if the First Amendment is somehow implicated by the Wisconsin statute, there are legitimate, content-neutral justifications for authorizing enhanced penalties for bias offenses which override any concern that free speech might be inhibited. Bias crimes are a criminologically distinct category of offenses that create special and quantifiable harms to society. . . .

States have clear interests, wholly unrelated to any expressive content associated with particular conduct, in targeting bias crimes for heightened penalties. As Justice [John Paul] Stevens stated in *R.A.V. v. St. Paul* (1992):

> Conduct that creates special risks or causes special harms may be prohibited by special rules. Lighting a fire near an ammunition dump or a gasoline storage tank is especially dangerous; such behavior may be punished more severely than burning trash in a vacant lot. Threatening someone because of her race or religious beliefs may cause particularly severe trauma or touch off a riot, and threatening a high public official may cause substantial social disruption, such threats may be punished more severely. . . .

Bias Crimes Are More Violent

Bias crimes are more violent than non-bias crimes. Indeed, bias crimes are at least three times more likely to involve criminal assault than non-bias crimes. These assaults are twice as likely to cause injury and four times more likely to result in hospitalization than non-bias assaults. Unlike crimes based on personal conflict or pecuniary gain, there is little a victim can do to lessen the severity of such an attack. Bias crime victims cannot easily appease an attacker by turning over property or by apologizing for past conduct. The violent purpose behind the crime generally eliminates the opportunity for a victim to lessen his or her injury through any meaningful act of compliance.

Bias crime assaults and homicides are not more severe solely because of the extent of the injuries, but also because of the depravity of the attacks. Victims are often not merely beaten, but severely tortured. For instance, during the first two weeks of 1993, an African-American tourist in Florida was doused with gasoline and set ablaze, while in California hate crime charges were filed in the case of a man who was beaten so severely that authorities could not even ascertain his race. Researchers, police and emergency medical professionals throughout the country recount with disturbing regularity multiple stab wounds and strikes, dismemberments, castrations, skull fractures, mutilations, strangulations and immolations suffered by bias assault victims. The Houston Police Department abandoned an undercover anti-gay hate crime decoy operation after only ten days because five officers were injured after being attacked with baseball bats, tree limbs and fists in four separate incidents.

Bias Crimes Are Random and Irrational

The irrational nature of bias crimes is particularly disruptive and threatening both to victims and to the community. Compared to conventional crimes, bias crimes are far more likely to be committed randomly against victims by complete strangers. Criminologists have concluded that there is far greater societal disruption from random acts of violence than there is from those violent acts which have some rational cause. The disruption to society is of enormous significance when whole groups of citizens are placed in constant fear of random violence from attackers with whom they have no direct connection.

Bias crimes are at least twice as likely to involve multiple offenders acting in concert, often against a single victim. Nationally, approximately 25% of violent crimes are committed by two or more offenders. An analysis of the jurisdictions having the most credible bias crime statistics reveals the disproportionate involvement of multiple offenders.

In Maryland, 71% of the bias crime cases involved multiple offenders. The comparable figures for New York City and Boston, respectively, were 75% and 64%. The Boston study reveals that most attacks involved four or more perpetrators and a lone victim. The conclusions of private researchers are in accord with these law enforcement figures. Numerous studies of large numbers of anti-gay cases, for example, reveal that multiple offender attacks account for between 48 to 78% of the victimizations. Such violent group conduct presents unique dangers because: (1) offenders are empowered by the heightened sense of dominance and exhilaration that results from group action; (2) individual offenders lose a sense of direct accountability for actions that occur at the hands of a group; and (3) the group offers anonymity. An analysis of lynchings in the first part of this century revealed that [as reported in the *New York Times*] "the larger the mob, the more atrocious and savage the lynching and the more likely [it is] to include burning or mutilating the victim." More recently, many of the most publicized bias homicides involved uncontrolled group attacks on lone victims. Such violence by disorderly crowds frequently results in more severe injuries, greater community disruption and a disproportionate diversion of scarce police resources.

Numerous well-respected studies find that a common characteristic of bias crimes is the presence of related serial victimizations, most of which go unreported. Two studies of Boston bias crimes revealed a pattern of multiple victimizations, starting with minor incidents which often lead to more serious offenses. In a 1986 study of racial, religious and ethnic victimizations the National Institute Against Prejudice and Violence revealed that 65% of victims experienced "multiple interconnected attacks," with an additional 17.5% experiencing multiple attacks in discrete incidents. Another influential study of anti-gay attacks revealed that 68% of those who had been threatened with violence and nearly half (47%) of those who had been physically assaulted reported multiple experiences of such episodes.

Conventional Statutes Are Inadequate

Clearly, conventional criminal statutes do not adequately deter bias crimes. Before the passage of Massachusetts' bias crime statute, the Boston Police Department consistently responded to repeat bias crimes committed either against the same victims, by the same perpetrators, or both. The first case prosecuted in the state under this statute involved a group of individuals whose members had been repeatedly arrested for committing criminal acts against the same group of minority families. After Boston began widespread enforcement of the statute, repeat incidents dropped significantly and the overall level of reported bias crimes in Boston fell by two-thirds. As the U.S. Commission on Civil Rights observed in a 1983 report:

> Effective police responses . . . are necessary to keep such [bias] incidents from spreading. If the police fail to respond or respond in ways that clearly demonstrate a lack of sensitivity, perpetrators can interpret the police inactivity as official sympathy or even sanction.

Risk of Social Disorder

The interchangeability of victims based merely upon perceived status heightens the social disruption associated with bias crimes. The substitutable nature of the victimization places entire classes of people on notice that they face a threat over which they have little meaningful control. The potential for conflict that flows from this characteristic of bias crimes creates particularly explosive situations, where one incident can lead to a series of related acts of random inter-group retaliation. A New York State task force [Governor's Task Force on Bias-Related Violence] recently concluded that "[a] single incident can be the tragedy of a lifetime to its victim and may be the spark that rends and disrupts an entire community."

Bias-related tensions, particularly those involving race, have consistently sparked this nation's most violent and disruptive civil disorders. Ample evidence illustrates how one incident can spark a series of incidents of random retaliation. The law enforcement data show that generally significant increases in the reported number of bias crimes within one city can be attributed to a large number of localized incidents or by an increase in the number of incidents occurring between members of two specific status groups involved in a trigger incident. These data indicate that a single incident can aggravate intergroup tensions and lead to a cycle of violent and criminal behavior.

Mitchell Was a Poorly Conceived Ruling

Jeffrey Rosen

Jeffrey Rosen writes on legal issues for the New Republic *magazine. A graduate of Harvard College and Yale Law School, he was a law clerk with the United States Court of Appeals. Rosen now teaches constitutional law at George Washington University.*

In the following essay Rosen takes a middle position on hate crime laws. He believes that they can be constitutional. However, criticisms based on civil liberties concerns are valid; hate crime laws that are loosely written or that are overly broad can endanger free speech. Rosen believes that the Wisconsin law in question was a well-written statute. However, he also holds that the opinion delivered by Chief Justice Rehnquist upholding the law was too dismissive of the concerns of civil libertarians. Rehnquist's opinion was too expansive, Rosen argues, leaving open the possibility that the Wisconsin law, while constitutional, could be applied in unconstitutional ways, thus endangering Americans' civil liberties.

I n every Supreme Court term, there is at least one case that tests, and vividly exposes, the character of the justices. . . . This year [1993] it is hate crimes. The outcome of *Wisconsin*

Jeffrey Rosen, "Bad Thoughts," *The New Republic,* July 5, 1993. Copyright © 1993 by The New Republic, Inc. Reproduced by permission.

v. Mitchell—which upheld a law that requires harsher sentences for criminals who "intentionally select" their victims "because of race, religion" and the like—was never really in doubt. But instead of being sensitive to the intricate First Amendment concerns that the case raised, [Chief Justice] William Rehnquist dismissed them contemptuously. His unanimous opinion reads like a lazy summary of the government's brief: polemical, self-assured and profoundly superficial. The fact that one of the justices wrote a separate concurrence suggests that none of them is concerned about policing the boundary between speech and conduct with analytical precision.

Hate Crimes Laws Must Be Carefully Crafted

Civil libertarians are familiar with the powerful policy arguments against hate crimes laws, which increase the punishment for behavior that is already criminal. But the constitutional arguments are far more complicated. A less cavalier opinion could have endorsed something like the ACLU's [American Civil Liberties Union] position: carefully crafted sentence enhancement laws, like Wisconsin's, may be constitutional. But sloppily drafted laws, like the one proposed by Representative Charles Schumer, which would ratchet up the sentences for crimes "in which the defendant's conduct was motivated by hatred, bias or prejudice," are unconstitutional. A comparison of the Wisconsin law, which the ACLU supports, and the Schumer bill, which it properly opposes, shows the importance of the distinctions that Rehnquist ignored.

The most important distinction is that the Wisconsin law does not formally require judges in hate crimes cases to determine whether the offender was motivated by bigoted thoughts. The Wisconsin law's language is identical to the wording of many federal civil rights statutes, such as the section of the U.S. Code that imposes penalties on any person who, by "threat of force," interferes with the constitutional rights of another person "because of his race, color, religion or national origin." And you can be prosecuted under the Wisconsin law— and the civil rights laws—even if you never utter a hateful word. One way of proving that a criminal selected his victims on the basis of race, for example, would be to introduce evidence that he attacked black people on different occasions and in different cities. . . .

Wisconsin Law Does Not Suppress Unpopular Ideas

Rehnquist's opinion clashes, in important ways, with the 1992 cross burning case, *RAV v. St. Paul.* By ignoring the key language in *RAV*—"special hostility toward the particular biases thus singled out . . . is precisely what the First Amendment forbids"—Rehnquist misses the most convincing way of distinguishing the two cases. Unlike the Schumer bill, and unlike most hate speech laws, the Wisconsin scheme is not, on its face, an attempt to suppress politically incorrect ideas. As [Justice] Clarence Thomas emphasized at the oral argument, you can be convicted under the Wisconsin law for intraracial as well as interracial violence. A black separatist who assaults a group of black attorneys for selling out would be no less liable than a white Klansmen who assaults an African American out of racism.

Nadine Strossen of the ACLU points to a final difference between the Wisconsin law and the Schumer bill. In Wisconsin the defendant's discriminatory intentions must be proved beyond a reasonable doubt. The Schumer bill, by contrast, contains no such requirement; and evidence of the defendant's bigoted thoughts—such as the fact that a neighbor heard he had a copy of *Mein Kampf*[1] on the bookshelf—can be admitted even if it is only tangentially related to the underlying

1. Adolf Hitler's racist book

crime. For the same reason, the ACLU has properly opposed Florida's law providing for an enhanced penalty if the crime "evidences prejudice."

If Rehnquist had focused narrowly on the formal neutrality of the Wisconsin law, in short, he could have upheld it in a way that distinguished it from laws that explicitly target bigotry. Instead, he was expansive. He invited legislatures to punish what he called "good" motivations more severely than "bad" ones; and in the process, he exacerbated First Amendment concerns rather than minimizing them. As Susan Gellman of the Ohio Public Defender's Office notes, if a state can increase the punishment for motivations it finds especially abhorrent, such as racism, then it can also decrease the punishment for motivations it finds less abhorrent, such as homophobia or opposition to abortion.

Rehnquist's Opinion Ignores Reasonable Objections

Rehnquist dismissed the First Amendment concerns in two laconic paragraphs. Treason, he noted, can depend on proving the defendant's bad motive; and in a 1947 case the Court allowed the government to introduce evidence of conversations that had taken place long before an indictment for treason because they cast light on the defendant's Nazi sympathies. Rehnquist's enthusiasm for a cold war treason opinion is startlingly insensitive. It slights what the Court had called, in an earlier case, "the concern uppermost in the framers' minds, that mere mental attitudes or expression should not be treason." And by going out of his way to compare hate crimes to treason, Rehnquist wrongly encourages the focus on politically unpopular views.

In the same spirit, Rehnquist belittles danger that the Wisconsin law—which increases the punishment for virtually every offense in the Wisconsin criminal code, from trespassing to adultery—can be applied in unconstitutional ways. "It is difficult," he writes sarcastically, "to conceive of a situation" where a minor misdemeanor, such as negligent operation of a motor vehicle, would be racially motivated. But other unconstitutional applications are not so difficult to conceive. The Wisconsin law threatens up to five years in jail for anyone who has sex with a married person "because of race," for example, bringing a ban on adultery perilously close to a ban on miscegenation. It creates a brand-new crime of group libel by increasing the punishment for race-based defamation. It would also require stiffer penalties for pro-choice protesters who trespass on the front lawn of a church "because of religion." Even the ACLU emphasizes that these cases raise "serious constitutional problems."

Trials May Become Ideological Witch-Hunts

Rehnquist also fails to acknowledge the powerful incentives to turn hate crimes trials into ideological witch-hunts, even when the language of the statutes is formally neutral. In Mitchell's case, the only evidence of his racial attitudes was the discussion about [the film] *Mississippi Burning,* which was not strictly necessary to prove that he selected his victim on the basis of race. But in other cases, defendants are encouraged to argue that their apparently racist conduct was not motivated by bigotry. A white man indicted under Ohio's similarly worded hate crimes law, for example, tried to prove he was not a bigot by emphasizing his "associations" with black friends and neighbors. This prompted the following remarkable cross-examination: "And you lived next door to [Mrs. Ware, a 65-year-old black neighbor] and you don't even know her first name?" No. "Never had dinner with her?" No. "Never invited her to a picnic at your house?" No. "I want you to name just one [black] person who was a really good friend of yours. . . ."

By slighting the danger that technically constitutional laws can be applied in unconstitutional ways, Rehnquist encourages legislatures to be similarly insensitive. As a result, the Anti Defamation League [ADL], whose model hate crimes statute has been followed in twenty-six states, no longer has an incentive to distinguish constitutional laws from clearly unconstitutional ones. "Before the *Mitchell* decision, we were planning to encourage states to follow the Wisconsin language. But the decision is so broad that I'm not sure we have to anymore," says Michael Lieberman, associate director of the ADL.

Why was no [Supreme Court] justice moved to write separately in this case? The charitable explanation is that all nine of them were so afraid of antagonizing their impatient and vindictive chief that they swallowed their doubts. The less charitable explanation is that no one cared enough about the delicate First Amendment issues to notice the distinctions that Rehnquist disparaged.

| "At issue [in the debate over hate crime laws] are two of the most elemental principles of American law, free speech and equal protection of the laws."

The Debate over Hate Crime Laws

John Spong

John Spong, a writer for Texas Monthly *magazine, specializes in Texas politics. The excerpt below covers the debate over hate crime laws, illustrating how state legislatures are dealing with the Supreme Court's decision in* Wisconsin v. Mitchell.

In 1998 the town of Jasper, Texas, was the scene of a vicious killing of a black man by three white supremacists. In response, some state legislators sought to pass a hate crime law. The debate in Texas, conducted after the 1993 Mitchell *decision, illustrates common themes in the hate crime controversy. Opponents of the hate crime laws worry that such laws could chill free speech. They also believe the laws deem some crime victims more worthy of protection than others, a practice that is inconsistent with the American ideal that all citizens are equal under the law. Proponents counter that hate crime laws protect certain citizens that have historically been victims of crimes because of their membership in despised groups. Hate crime legislation was passed in Texas in 2002.*

T he James Byrd, Jr., Hate Crimes Act, named for the Jasper resident who was dragged to death behind a pickup truck

John Spong, "The Hate Debate," *Texas Monthly,* April 2001. Copyright © 2001 by *Texas Monthly.* Reproduced by permission.

in 1998 by three white supremacists, increases the punishment for crimes whose victims were targeted because of their race, religion, or sexual preference. Passions were first aroused by the impending death in a Senate committee of the 1999 version of the bill, sending senators into closed-door party caucuses for hours of deadlock and dissension. Last year [2000] the National Association for the Advancement of Colored People galvanized African American voters against presidential candidate George W. Bush with a TV spot alluding to the dragging death of Byrd and blaming Bush, who had expressed reservations about the bill, for its defeat. And the passions surfaced again in a hearing on the Byrd bill before the House Judicial Affairs Committee.

Stella Byrd, the victim's mother, pleaded with the committee to make the bill a testament against hate that would show her son's children that their father had not died in vain. But then a retired Air Force major testified about being spat on after returning from Vietnam and asked why people who hate the military should not be prosecuted under the bill. And state representative Will Hartnett, a Dallas Republican who is the vice chairman of the committee considering the bill, asked why state law should treat the rape of one six-year-old girl differently from the rape of any other six-year-old girl. . . .

Equality Under the Law

Most lawmaking involves familiar questions of politics and policy, matters that are worth fighting over but are nevertheless well removed from basic ideas of what kind of society we want and what role our laws should play in shaping it. There is a certain amount of government intrusion when the state sets a speed limit or requires cars to be inspected, but it does not have the same impact as a law that says society disapproves of a certain thought or belief, or one that says that some victims need more protection than others from similar crimes. Hate crimes laws seem to draw just these sorts of lines, which is one reason they stir up so much emotion. At issue are two of the most elemental principles of American law, free speech and equal protection of the laws, the kinds of things that first-year law students argue about among themselves in the first week of law school. The hate crimes debate reminds me of the arguments my classmates and I used to make: Opponents of hate crimes protections say that the Law should treat all people the same. Proponents acknowledge that as true, but ask where, in a world in which people do not treat each other the same, can a victim turn but to the Law?

The proponents believe that a hate crime is fundamentally different from an otherwise identical crime that lacks the element of hate. Defacing property is a crime, but there is a difference between kids spray-painting "Seniors Rule!" on the wall of a high school cafeteria and kids spray-painting a swastika on the wall of a synagogue, and the difference should be reflected in greater punishment for the crime that is accompanied by hate: a class C misdemeanor (maximum fine of $500 and no jail time) for "Seniors Rule!" but a class B misdemeanor (maximum fine of $2,000 and up to 180 days in jail) for the swastika. But Cathie Adams, the president of the Dallas-based Eagle Forum, a conservative political group, insists that there is no distinction. "Look, I am willing to fall on my sword for the Jews," she told me. "I've been to Israel over twenty times, and I have lobbied for continuing to send aid to the Israelis, which surprises a lot of my friends. But graffiti is graffiti."

Punishing Thought

The justification for the harsher sentence is that a crime inspired by hate has a different effect than ordinary vandalism, both in the way it is felt in the victim's community and in the community at large. The difference is intended by the perpetrator and deserves a different response from society. Imagine the feelings, from fear to anger, created among African Americans in Jasper by what happened to James Byrd, Jr., and the shame and onus that fell upon the entire town. (The Byrd bill, however, does not apply to first-degree felonies or capital crimes, for reasons presidential candidate Bush pointed out during a debate with Al Gore: "[W]e can't enhance the penalty any more than putting those three thugs to death. And that's what's going to happen in the state of Texas"—except that Bush had it wrong. Only two of the three defendants received the death penalty; the third got a life sentence.) The toughest hurdle for hate crimes laws is that while the effect of the swastika and "Seniors Rule!" may be markedly distinct, the only real difference between the acts themselves is the thought behind them. "It's penalizing people for what the government thinks they thought when they committed the crime, based on the fact that society doesn't understand that way of thinking," says Kelly Shackelford, the president of Plano's Free Market Foundation of Texas, a conservative political group. "But you've got to let people engage in free speech in political debate, even if you don't like what they say."

State representative [Senfronia] Thompson's answer is: "You want to call me all kinds of names? Call me a no-good, low-down, dirty nigger? Help yourself. But the minute you hit me, you better look out, because it becomes something else."

Court Cases Distinguish Speech from Act

The U.S. Supreme Court agrees that hate speech by itself cannot be punished. In *R.A.V. v. St. Paul,* a 1992 case, the Court struck down a city ordinance prohibiting hate speech saying, among other things, that a burning cross is an expression of a political belief and as such is protected by the First Amendment. But the Court has also upheld punishment-enhancement laws like the proposed Byrd bill. In *Wisconsin v. Mitchell,* a 1993 case, Chief Justice William Rehnquist wrote for a unanimous Court that while the thought itself may be protected, once it became the motive for a crime and the crime was put into action, the thought became something more than just an idea. It became active discrimination. Rehnquist drew an analogy to unemployment cases. The boss can dislike someone for racial or religious reasons—the thought is protected from a discrimination lawsuit—but to fire the person for those reasons would not be protected. Ironically, the Wisconsin case involved a conviction under the hate crimes statute for a black kid who led an attack on a white kid.

Yet proving that the forbidden thought exists may cause some problems. "Imagine someone is charged with a hate crime against a gay person," says University of Texas law professor Douglas Laycock. "Can the prosecutor bring up where the defendant goes to church, what kind of sermons he is listening to, how his church feels about homosexuality?" Presumably the answer is no, unless the prosecutor can show some relationship between those beliefs and the actual attack. The courts have made some distinctions here: In a Texas case, circumstantial evidence was good enough to prove a hate crime had been committed when an attacker called his victim a "nigger" before, during, and after beating him up and called people who tried to help the victim "nigger lovers." But the U.S. Supreme Court has upheld a lower court decision that membership in the Aryan Brotherhood [a white supremacist prison gang] was not by itself enough to establish that a white defendant's attack of a black person was racially motivated.

Special Victims

The equal-protection argument against the hate crimes bill is based on the fact that the bill provides some citizens with greater protection—that is, the longer prison sentence provides a greater deterrent to spitting on an African American than on a Vietnam veteran. The harsher penalty suggests that a greater value is being placed on the loss incurred by certain victims. Inevitably, the critics ask, if a man and his wife walk down the street together and are attacked by a misogynist, does the woman's injury count for more than the man's? A similar argument was made during a [Texas] House debate on the hate crimes bill in 1999 by Representative Suzanna Gratia Hupp of Lampas, and it was no law school hypothetical: Her parents were killed in the tragic 1991 shooting at the Luby's Cafeteria in Killeen by a man apparently acting out of a hatred of women. But supporters of the bill pointed out that the Legislature makes distinctions between victims all the time. The state's definition of injury to a child makes it a more serious offense to injure a child who is 6 years and 364 days old than a child who is 7 years and 1 day old. Assaulting a public servant is a more serious offense than assaulting someone who bumps into you on the street.

Of course, if the Byrd bill singled out specific groups for protection—say, African Americans, Jews, and homosexuals—the equal-protection concerns of the Fourteenth Amendment would come into play. But the Byrd bill's authors avoided that trap. It protects victims singled out because of religion, not Jewishness. Fundamentalist Baptists who are terrorized by pro-choicers would get the same protection as Jews assaulted by members of the Aryan Brotherhood.

Protecting Historically Oppressed Groups

Why shouldn't the law simply define a hate crime as one committed against a member of any group the perpetrator despises? That was the approach of the current Texas hate crimes law, passed in 1993 in response to the defacement of synagogues. The law enhanced penalties for crimes targeting victims identified by membership "in" a group. This presumably would have covered the Vietnam vet who was spat on or student athletes who were targets at the Columbine shooting and who a legislator wanted to protect in 1999. But by incorporating any group, the law became so vague that prosecutors considered it unenforceable. Each subsequent session, proponents have sought to clarify which victims are protected: those selected for their race, religion, or sexual orientation. The bill recognizes these broad categories, not specific groups within them such as African Americans, Jews, and homosexuals. If militant Jews were to terrorize a fundamentalist Baptist, they would fall under the proposed hate crimes law—as they should. The final reason for limiting the categories to race, creed, or sexual preference is that hate crimes most often involve these categories. It's not that high school athletes don't deserve protection; it's that they historically have not needed it.

In contrast to the philosophical battle over the hate crimes bill, the political issue is simple. Most of the opposition comes from Republicans, and for many Republicans, the inclusion of sexual orientation is the main reason for opposing the bill. The more-conservative element of their party opposes legal rights for homosexuals and worry that by implicitly singling out gays and lesbians for protection, the hate crimes bill could become the first step in a landslide of gay rights and recognition. A vote for hate crimes legislation could be politically perilous in a Republican primary. Philosophical issues notwithstanding, if sexual preference were taken out of the bill, leaving only race and creed, the law would likely pass. . . .

As for the legal arguments, both sides are absolutely convinced that they are right. Where the proponents have the edge is in symbolism. That case was made most eloquently by state representative Patti Sadler of Henderson during the 1999 House debate. "There are votes and bills that tell the world who we are, what we value, what we cherish, what we believe in. . . . We can't end hatred and violence and bias and prejudice, but it is our duty to punish conduct that we find reprehensible; conduct that we believe is wrong. And who of you will stand and tell me that conduct based on hatred and bias and prejudice is anything but wrong?"

CHAPTER 4

Legalizing Racial Preferences in College Admissions

Chapter Preface

Case Overview: *Grutter v. Bollinger* (2003)

Barbara Grutter, a white Michigan resident, applied to the University of Michigan Law School in 1996. A forty-three-year-old successful businesswoman, Grutter thought she would bring a unique set of skills and opinions to the law school's student body. She was initially placed on a waiting list for enrollment, but eventually her application was rejected. When Grutter discovered that several African American students had gained admission with test scores and grade point averages below hers, she contacted her state representative. The representative advised her to contact the Center for Individual Rights, a public interest law firm. The firm agreed to take her case, and together they brought suit against the law school and Lee Bollinger, president of the University of Michigan.

Barbara Grutter's suit alleged that race was the predominant factor in the decision to reject her application. Her lawyers argued that certain minority groups had "significantly greater chance of admission than students with similar credentials from disfavored racial groups." Grutter sought an end to admissions practices that discriminate on the basis of race as well as an injunction ordering the University of Michigan Law School to admit her. At her trial in the District Court for the Eastern District of Michigan, where testimony from both parties was heard, Grutter prevailed and was granted an injunction to be admitted to the law school. However, the court of appeals reversed the district court's ruling, and the case went to the U.S. Supreme Court.

Arguing before the Court, the University of Michigan cited the need to create a "critical mass" of minority students at the law school. In order to accomplish this goal, the law school needed to consider race as a "plus factor" in evaluating applications from members of underrepresented minorities. The law school stressed that this policy was arrived at in accord with the *Regents of the University of California v. Bakke* decision (1978), which found that the state had a "compelling interest" in having a diverse student body. Grutter's attorneys countered that whites were significantly disadvantaged to the point where an African American applicant with similar credentials to a white applicant was hundreds of times more likely to gain admission. Therefore, this practice failed the "strict scrutiny" test, which requires race-based policies to be narrowly tailored to meet a specific "compelling interest."

The Court decided that the University of Michigan Law School's policy was constitutional because it took race into account without employing a point system or quotas. By contrast, in *Gratz v. Bollinger,* a companion case to *Grutter,* the Court struck down the University of Michigan's method for considering race among its undergraduate applicants because that system awarded points to applicants based on their race. In deciding *Grutter,* the Court agreed with the school's claim that it needed to create a "critical mass" of underrepresented minority students. The Court held that top law schools must be open to people of all ethnicities. In an increasingly diverse America, said Justice Sandra Day O'Connor in her majority opinion, the legitimacy of American leadership depends on all ethnicities being represented. Because much of that leadership is drawn from top law schools such as the University of Michigan's, these schools must admit members of underrepresented minorities, even if they have lower standardized test scores and grade point averages than whites. O'Connor's opinion enshrined the concept of "diversity" into constitutional law.

"Universities can . . . consider race or ethnicity . . . [in] consideration of each and every applicant."

The Court's Opinion: Racial Preferences Are Permitted in College Admissions

Sandra Day O'Connor

Sandra Day O'Connor was the first female justice of the Supreme Court. A graduate of Stanford Law School, she served on the Supreme Court from 1981 to 2005. During her time on the Court she was considered a pivotal "swing-vote," sometimes agreeing with the Court's conservatives such as Chief Justice William Rehnquist, other times siding with liberals such as Justice John Paul Stevens.

O'Connor is the author of the majority opinion in the Grutter v. Bollinger *case, excerpted here. She bases her opinion on the Court's* Regents of the University of California v. Bakke *opinion (1978). The author of that opinion, Lewis Powell, recognized "a compelling state interest" in creating an ethnically diverse student body at institutions of higher learning. Powell focused his opinion on the educational setting, claiming that diversity promoted a "robust exchange of ideas." O'Connor, in the* Grutter *decision, extends the "compelling interest" argument. Citing briefs from business, educational, religious, and military organizations, she holds that American society's increasing diversity requires that various ethnic groups be represented in institutions such as law schools. In order to meet that goal, institutions*

Sandra Day O'Connor, majority opinion, *Grutter v. Bollinger,* U.S. Supreme Court, 2003.

must be able to take race and ethnic background into account when considering whom to admit.

T he [University of Michigan] Law School's educational judgment that [racial] diversity is essential to its educational mission is one to which we defer. The Law school's assessment that diversity will, in fact, yield educational benefits is substantiated by respondents and their amici.[1] Our scrutiny of the interest asserted by the Law School is no less strict for taking into account complex educational judgments in an area that lies primarily within the expertise of the university. Our holding today is in keeping with our tradition of giving a degree of deference to a university's academic decisions, within constitutionally prescribed limits.

We have long recognized that, given the important purpose of public education and the expansive freedoms of speech and thought associated with the university environment, universities occupy a special niche in our constitutional tradition. In announcing the principle of student body diversity as a compelling state interest, Justice [Lewis F.] Powell invoked our cases recognizing a constitutional dimension, grounded in the First Amendment, of educational autonomy: "The freedom of a university to make its own judgments as to education includes the selection of its student body." [*Regents of the University of California v. Bakke* (1978).] From this premise, Justice Powell reasoned that by claiming "the right to select those students who will contribute the most to the 'robust exchange of ideas,'" a university "seek[s] to achieve a goal that is of paramount importance in the fulfillment of its mission." Our conclusion that the Law School has a compelling interest in a diverse student body is informed by our view that attaining a diverse student body is at the heart of the Law School's proper

---

1. amici curiae—literally, "friends of the court" (singular: amicus curiae); third parties who present arguments, called briefs, in favor of one side or another in a court case

institutional mission, and that "good faith" on the part of a university is "presumed" absent "a showing to the contrary."

Enrolling a Critical Mass

As part of its goal of "assembling a class that is both exceptionally academically qualified and broadly diverse," the Law School seeks to "enroll a 'critical mass' of minority students." The Law School's interest is not simply "to assure within its student body some specified percentage of a particular group merely because of its race or ethnic origin." [*Bakke*.] That would amount to outright racial balancing, which is patently unconstitutional. Rather, the Law School's concept of critical mass is defined by reference to the educational benefits that diversity is designed to produce.

These benefits are substantial. As the District Court emphasized, the Law School's admissions policy promotes "cross-racial understanding," helps to break down racial stereotypes, and "enables [students] to better understand persons of different races." These benefits are "important and laudable," because "classroom discussion is livelier, more spirited, and simply more enlightening and interesting" when the students have "the greatest possible variety of backgrounds."

The Law School's claim of a compelling interest is further bolstered by its amici, who point to the educational benefits that flow from student body diversity. In addition to the expert studies and reports entered into evidence at trial, numerous studies show that student body diversity promotes learning outcomes, and "better prepares students for an increasingly diverse workforce and society, and better prepares them as professionals." [Brief for American Educational Research Association et al. as amicus curiae.]

These benefits are not theoretical but real, as major American businesses have made clear that the skills needed in today's increasingly global marketplace can only be developed through exposure to widely diverse people, cultures, ideas, and viewpoints. What is more, high-ranking retired officers and civilian leaders of the United States military assert that, "[b]ased on [their] decades of experience," a "highly qualified, racially diverse officer corps ... is essential to the military's ability to fulfill its principal mission to provide national security." [Brief for Julius W. Becton Jr. et al. as amici curiae.] The primary sources for the Nation's officer corps are the service academies and the Reserve Officers Training Corps (ROTC), the latter comprising students already admitted to participating colleges and universities. At present, "the military cannot achieve an officer corps that is both highly qualified and racially diverse unless the service academies and the ROTC use limited race-conscious recruiting and admissions policies." [Brief for Becton Jr.] To fulfill its mission, the military "must be selective in admissions for training and education for the officer corps, and it must train and educate a highly qualified, racially diverse officer corps in a racially diverse setting." [Brief for Becton Jr.] We agree that "[i]t requires only a small step from this analysis to conclude that our country's other most selective institutions must remain both diverse and selective." [Brief for Becton Jr.]

We have repeatedly acknowledged the overriding importance of preparing students for work and citizenship, describing education as pivotal to "sustaining our political and cultural heritage" with a fundamental role in maintaining the fabric of society. [*Plyler v. Doe* (1982).] This Court has long recognized that "education ... is the very foundation of good citizenship." [*Brown v. Board of Education* (1954).] For this reason, the diffusion of knowledge and opportunity through public institutions of higher education must be accessible to all individuals regardless of race or ethnicity. The United States, as amicus curiae, affirms that "[e]nsuring that public institutions are open and available to all segments of American society, including people of all races and ethnicities, represents a paramount government objective." And, "[n]owhere is the importance of such openness more acute than in the context of higher education." [Brief for United States.] Effective participation by members of all racial and ethnic groups in the civic life of our Nation is essential if the dream of one Nation, indivisible, is to be realized.

Top Law Schools Produce the Nation's Leaders

Moreover, universities, and in particular, law schools, represent the training ground for a large number of our Nation's leaders. Individuals with law degrees occupy roughly half the state governorships, more than half the seats in the United States Senate, and more than a third of the seats in the United States House of Representatives. The pattern is even more striking when it comes to highly selective law schools. A handful of these schools accounts for 25 of the 100 United States Senators, 74 United States Courts of Appeals judges, and nearly 200 of the more than 600 United States District Court judges.

In order to cultivate a set of leaders with legitimacy in the eyes of the citizenry, it is necessary that the path to leadership be visibly open to talented and qualified individuals of every race and ethnicity. All members of our heterogeneous society must have confidence in the openness and integrity of the educational institutions that provide this training. As we have recognized, law schools "cannot be effective in isolation from the individuals and institutions with which the law interacts." [*Sweatt v. Painter.*] Access to legal education (and thus the legal profession) must be inclusive of talented and qualified individuals of every race and ethnicity, so that all members of our heterogeneous society may participate in the educational institutions that provide the training and education necessary to succeed in America.

The Law School does not premise its need for critical mass on "any belief that minority students always (or even consistently) express some characteristic minority viewpoint on any issue." [Brief for Respondent Bollinger et al.] To the contrary, diminishing the force of such stereotypes is both a crucial part of the Law School's mission, and one that it cannot accomplish with only token numbers of minority students. Just as growing up in a particular region or having particular professional experiences is likely to affect an individual's views, so too is one's own, unique experience of being a racial minority in a society, like our own, in which race unfortunately still matters. The Law School has determined, based on its experience and expertise, that a "critical mass" of underrepresented minorities is necessary to further its compelling interest in securing the educational benefits of a diverse student body.

A Narrowly Tailored Plan

Even in the limited circumstance when drawing racial distinctions is permissible to further a compelling state interest, government is still "constrained in how it may pursue that end: [T]he means chosen to accomplish the [government's] asserted purpose must be specifically and narrowly framed to accomplish that purpose." [*Shaw v. Hunt* (1996).] The purpose of the narrow tailoring requirement is to ensure that "the means chosen 'fit' . . . th[e] compelling goal so closely that there is little or no possibility that the motive for the classification was illegitimate racial prejudice or stereotype." [*Richmond v. J.A. Croson Co.* (1989).]

Since *Bakke*, we have had no occasion to define the contours of the narrow-tailoring inquiry with respect to race-conscious university admissions programs. That inquiry must be calibrated to fit the distinct issues raised by the use of race to achieve student body diversity in public higher education. Contrary to Justice [Anthony M.] Kennedy's assertions, we do not "abandon strict scrutiny." Rather, as we have already explained, we adhere to *Adarand*'s teaching that the very purpose of strict scrutiny is to take such "relevant differences into account." [*Adarand Constructors v. Peña* (1995).]

To be narrowly tailored, a race-conscious admissions program cannot use a quota system—it cannot "insulat[e] each category of applicants with certain desired qualifications from competition with all other applicants." [*Bakke.*] Instead, a university may consider race or ethnicity only as a "'plus' in a particular applicant's file," without "insulat[ing] the individual from comparison with all other candidates for the available seats." [*Bakke.*] In other words, an admissions program must be "flexible enough to consider all pertinent elements of diversity in light of the particular qualifications of each applicant, and to place them on the same footing for consideration, although not necessarily according them the same weight." [*Bakke.*]

We find that the Law School's admissions program bears the hallmarks of a narrowly tailored plan. As Justice Powell made clear in *Bakke,* truly individualized consideration demands that race be used in a flexible, nonmechanical way. It follows from this mandate that universities cannot establish quotas for members of certain racial groups or put members of those groups on separate admissions tracks. Nor can universities insulate applicants who belong to certain racial or ethnic groups from the competition for admission. Universities can, however, consider race or ethnicity more flexibly as a "plus" factor in the context of individualized consideration of each and every applicant.

We are satisfied that the Law School's admissions program, like the Harvard plan described by Justice Powell, does not operate as a quota. Properly understood, a "quota" is a program in which a certain fixed number or proportion of opportunities are "reserved exclusively for certain minority groups." [*Richmond v. J.A. Croson Co.*] Quotas "'impose a fixed number or percentage which must be attained, or which cannot be exceeded,'" [*Sheet Metal Workers v. EEOC* (1986).]

and "insulate the individual from comparison with all other candidates for the available seats." [*Bakke.*] In contrast, "a permissible goal . . . require[s] only a good-faith effort . . . to come within a range demarcated by the goal itself," [*Sheet Metal Workers v. EEOC*], and permits consideration of race as a "plus" factor in any given case while still ensuring that each candidate "compete[s] with all other qualified applicants." [*Johnson v. Transportation Agency* (1987).]

> "I do not believe that the Constitu-
> tion gives the Law School such free
> rein in the use of race."

Dissenting Opinion: Racial Balancing in College Admissions Is Unconstitutional

William H. Rehnquist

William H. Rehnquist was appointed to the Supreme Court in 1971 and was made chief justice in 1986. He served as chief justice until his death in 2005. He was known as a conservative but was more widely hailed for his administrative skills than for the opinions he issued.

In his dissent in Grutter v. Bollinger, *excerpted here, Rehnquist analyzes the logic of the University of Michigan Law School's claim that it has an interest in having a "critical mass" of students from underrepresented minority groups. He shows that the actual numbers of minority admissions vary from group to group, from as low as thirteen for Native Americans to around one hundred for African Americans. In order to achieve "critical mass," he posits, admissions for each ethnic group should be approximately equal in number. Rehnquist goes on to suggest that the numbers admitted from each minority group correspond closely with that group's percentage of applicants, leading him to claim that the school is trying to match the percentage of acceptances with the percentage of applicants for each ethnic group.*

William H. Rehnquist, dissenting opinion, *Grutter v. Bollinger,* U.S. Supreme Court, 2003.

Such a racial balancing system, he concludes, violates the equal protection clause of the Fourteenth Amendment.

I agree with the Court [in *Grutter v. Bollinger*] that, "in the limited circumstance when drawing racial distinctions is permissible," the government must ensure that its means are narrowly tailored to achieve a compelling state interest. I do not believe, however, that the University of Michigan Law School's (Law School) means are narrowly tailored to the interest it asserts. The Law School claims it must take the steps it does to achieve a "'critical mass'" of underrepresented minority students. But its actual program bears no relation to this asserted goal. Stripped of its "critical mass" veil, the Law School's program is revealed as a naked effort to achieve racial balancing.

Race-Based Policies Require Strict Scrutiny

As we have explained many times, "[a]ny preference based on racial or ethnic criteria must necessarily receive a most searching examination." [*Adarand Constructors, Inc. v. Peña* (1995).] Our cases establish that, in order to withstand this demanding inquiry, respondents must demonstrate that their methods of using race "'fit'" a compelling state interest "with greater precision than any alternative means." [*Adarand.*]

Before the Court's decision today, we consistently applied the same strict scrutiny analysis regardless of the government's purported reason for using race and regardless of the setting in which race was being used. We rejected calls to use more lenient review in the face of claims that race was being used in "good faith" because "[m]ore than good motives should be required when government seeks to allocate its resources by way of an explicit racial classification system." [*Adarand.*] We likewise rejected calls to apply more lenient review based on the particular setting in which race is being used. Indeed, even in the specific context of higher education, we emphasized that "constitutional limitations protecting individual rights may not be disregarded." [*University of California Regents v. Bakke* (1978).]

Although the Court recites the language of our strict scrutiny analysis, its application of that review is unprecedented in its deference.

Defining "Critical Mass"

Respondents' [Bollinger et al.] asserted justification for the Law School's use of race in the admissions process is "obtaining 'the educational benefits that flow from a diverse student body.'" They contend that a "critical mass" of underrepresented minorities is necessary to further that interest. Respondents and school administrators explain generally that "critical mass" means a sufficient number of underrepresented minority students to achieve several objectives: To ensure that these minority students do not feel isolated or like spokespersons for their race; to provide adequate opportunities for the type of interaction upon which the educational benefits of diversity depend; and to challenge all students to think critically and reexamine stereotypes. These objectives indicate that "critical mass" relates to the size of the student body. Respondents further claim that the Law School is achieving "critical mass."

In practice, the Law School's program bears little or no relation to its asserted goal of achieving "critical mass." Respondents explain that the Law School seeks to accumulate a "critical mass" of *each* underrepresented minority group. But the record demonstrates that the Law School's admissions practices with respect to these groups differ dramatically and cannot be defended under any consistent use of the term "critical mass."

From 1995 through 2000, the Law School admitted between 1,130 and 1,310 students. Of those, between 13 and 19 were Native American, between 91 and 108 were African-Americans, and between 47 and 56 were Hispanic. If the Law

139

School is admitting between 91 and 108 African-Americans in order to achieve "critical mass," thereby preventing African-American students from feeling "isolated or like spokespersons for their race," one would think that a number of the same order of magnitude would be necessary to accomplish the same purpose for Hispanics and Native Americans. Similarly, even if all of the Native American applicants admitted in a given year matriculate, which the record demonstrates is not at all the case, how can this possibly constitute a "critical mass" of Native Americans in a class of over 350 students? In order for this pattern of admission to be consistent with the Law School's explanation of "critical mass," one would have to believe that the objectives of "critical mass" offered by respondents are achieved with only half the number of Hispanics and one-sixth the number of Native Americans as compared to African-Americans. But respondents offer no race-specific reasons for such disparities. Instead, they simply emphasize the importance of achieving "critical mass," without any explanation of why that concept is applied differently among the three underrepresented minority groups.

Different Groups Treated Differently

These different numbers, moreover, come only as a result of substantially different treatment among the three underrepresented minority groups, as is apparent in an example offered by the Law School and highlighted by the Court: The school asserts that it "frequently accepts nonminority applicants with grades and test scores lower than underrepresented minority applicants (and other nonminority applicants) who are rejected." Specifically, the Law School states that "[s]ixty-nine minority applicants were rejected between 1995 and 2000 with at least a 3.5 [grade point average (GPA)] and a [score of] 159 or higher on the [Law School Admissions Test (LSAT)]" while a number of Caucasian and Asian-American applicants with similar or lower scores were admitted.

Review of the record reveals only 67 such individuals. Of these 67 individuals, 56 were Hispanic, while only 6 were African-American, and only 5 were Native American. This discrepancy reflects a consistent practice. For example, in 2000, 12 Hispanics who scored between a 159–160 on the LSAT and earned a GPA of 3.00 or higher applied for admission and only 2 were admitted. Meanwhile, 12 African-Americans in the same range of qualifications applied for admission and all 12 were admitted. Likewise, that same year, 16 Hispanics who scored between a 151–153 on the LSAT and earned a 3.00 or higher applied for admission and only 1 of those applicants was admitted. Twenty-three similarly qualified African-Americans applied for admission and 14 were admitted.

These statistics have a significant bearing on petitioner's case. Respondents have *never* offered any race-specific arguments explaining why significantly more individuals from one underrepresented minority group are needed in order to achieve "critical mass" or further student body diversity. They certainly have not explained why Hispanics, who they have said are among "the groups most isolated by racial barriers in our country," should have their admission capped out in this manner. True, petitioner is neither Hispanic nor Native American. But the Law School's disparate admissions practices with respect to these minority groups demonstrate that its alleged goal of "critical mass" is simply a sham. Petitioner may use these statistics to expose this sham, which is the basis for the Law School's admission of less qualified underrepresented minorities in preference to her. Surely strict scrutiny cannot permit these sorts of disparities without at least some explanation.

Admissions Numbers Show Racial Balancing

Only when the "critical mass" label is discarded does a likely explanation for these numbers emerge. The Court states that the Law School's goal of attaining a "critical mass" of underrepresented minority students is not an interest in merely "assur[ing] within its student body some specified percentage of a particular group merely because of its race or ethnic origin." The Court recognizes that such an interest "would amount to outright racial balancing, which is patently unconstitutional." The Court concludes, however, that the Law School's use of race in admissions, consistent with Justice [Lewis] Powell's opinion in *Bakke*, only pays "[s]ome attention to numbers."

But the correlation between the percentage of the Law School's pool of applicants who are members of the three minority groups and the percentage of the admitted applicants who are members of these same groups is far too precise to be dismissed as merely the result of the school paying "some attention to [the] numbers." . . .

For example, in 1995, when 9.7% of the applicant pool was African-American, 9.4% of the admitted class was African-American. By 2000, only 7.5% of the applicant pool was African-American, and 7.3% of the admitted class was African-American. This correlation is striking. Respondents themselves emphasize that the number of underrepresented minority students admitted to the Law School would be significantly smaller if the race of each applicant were not considered. But, as the examples above illustrate, the measure of the decrease would differ dramatically among the groups. The tight correlation between the percentage of applicants and admittees of a given race, therefore, must result from careful race based planning by the Law School. It suggests a formula for admission based on the aspirational assumption that all applicants are equally qualified academically, and therefore that the proportion of each group admitted should be the same as the proportion of that group in the applicant pool.

Not only do respondents fail to explain this phenomenon, they attempt to obscure it. But the divergence between the percentages of underrepresented minorities in the applicant pool and in the *enrolled* classes is not the only relevant comparison. In fact, it may not be the most relevant comparison. The Law School cannot precisely control which of its admitted applicants decide to attend the university. But it can and, as the numbers demonstrate, clearly does employ racial preferences in extending offers of admission. Indeed, the ostensibly flexible nature of the Law School's admissions program that the Court finds appealing appears to be, in practice, a carefully managed program designed to ensure proportionate representation of applicants from selected minority groups.

I do not believe that the Constitution gives the Law School such free rein in the use of race. The Law School has offered no explanation for its actual admissions practices and, unexplained, we are bound to conclude that the Law School has managed its admissions program, not to achieve a "critical mass," but to extend offers of admission to members of selected minority groups in proportion to their statistical representation in the applicant pool. But this is precisely the type of racial balancing that the Court itself calls "patently unconstitutional."

Race-Based Admissions Lack Time Limit

Finally, I believe that the Law School's program fails strict scrutiny because it is devoid of any reasonably precise time limit on the Law School's use of race in admissions. We have emphasized that we will consider "the planned duration of the remedy" in determining whether a race-conscious program is constitutional. [*Fullilove v. Klitznick* (1980).] . . . Our previous cases have required some limit on the duration of programs such as this because discrimination on the basis of race is invidious.

The Court suggests a possible 25-year limitation on the Law School's current program. Respondents, on the other hand, remain more ambiguous, explaining that "the Law School of course recognizes that race-conscious programs must have reasonable durational limits, and the Sixth Circuit properly found such a limit in the Law School's resolve to cease considering race when genuine race-neutral alternatives become available." These discussions of a time limit are the vaguest of assurances. In truth, they permit the Law School's use of racial preferences on a seemingly permanent basis. Thus, an important component of strict scrutiny—that a program be limited in time—is casually subverted.

The Court, in an unprecedented display of deference under our strict scrutiny analysis, upholds the Law School's program despite its obvious flaws. We have said that when it comes to the use of race, the connection between the ends and the means used to attain them must be precise. But here the flaw is deeper than that; it is not merely a question of "fit" between ends and means. Here the means actually used are forbidden by the Equal Protection Clause of the Constitution.

*"Equal protection, as an individual
civil right, is imploded when you elevate diversity to a compelling state
interest."*

Race-Based College
Admissions Violate
Individual Rights

A. Lee Parks Jr.

*A. Lee Parks Jr. is a lawyer and partner in the firm of Parks,
Chesin and Walbert in Atlanta, Georgia. In 2000 he filed a lawsuit on behalf of white applicants to the University of Georgia,
alleging they were denied admission because of an affirmative
action quota system. He won that case, with a federal appeals
court ruling that Georgia's system of awarding additional points
for belonging to an underrepresented minority group violated
terms of the 1964 Civil Rights Act.*

*In the following selection, written in 2003 as if he were argu-
ing before the U.S. Supreme Court, Parks attacks the goal of racial diversity in admissions to institutions of higher education.
He contends that in* Grutter v. Bollinger *and* Gratz v. Bollinger,
*both of which involved consideration of the race of applicants in
the college admissions process, the rights of nonminority individuals have been violated. Programs that put diversity ahead of
individual merit conflict with the American constitutional tradition, which vindicates the rights of individuals over group rights.
Those arguing for diversity seek a collective right of members of*

145

racial or ethnic minorities to a certain number of admissions to institutions of higher learning. The plaintiff in Grutter *seeks to defend her right to be judged on her individual achievements alone. Park argues that in cases where group and individual rights conflict, individual rights must prevail.*

I n the *Gratz* and *Grutter* cases, the Court will finally decide the legality under Title VI of the Civil Rights Act of 1964, and the constitutionality under the 14th Amendment, of an admissions policy that is programmed to admit a predetermined percentage of minority applicants. The University of Michigan seeks constitutional footing for its admitted preference of African-American and Hispanic undergraduate and law-school applicants based on the contention that racial diversity makes for a better education—and that adequate racial diversity can't be achieved without rejecting a certain number of more academically qualified white applicants in favor of preferred minority applicants.

Group Rights Versus Individual Rights

Historically, our Constitution has compelled the courts to vindicate the civil rights of the individual when a government has sought to subordinate them to so-called rights of the collective. The question before your Honors today is whether Justice Lewis F. Powell Jr.'s concurring opinion in the 1978 *Regents of the University of California v. Bakke* decision was a binding Supreme Court precedent for the proposition that racial diversity in higher education is such a compelling state interest that the group rights of minority applicants can trump the individual civil rights of more academically qualified white students. In a nutshell, reconciling the individual-versus collective-rights conundrum that well-meaning governmental efforts at social engineering usually generate is what the flap about "diversity" is fundamentally about. . . .

Diversity Policies Are Ineffective and Illegal

Michigan freely admits that its use of race as an admissions factor does not achieve any remedial purpose. Under this Court's binding precedent, that honest confession should end the constitutional inquiry because, as noted in *Hopwood* "Diversity fosters, rather than minimizes, the use of race."

Several circuit courts have applied the strict-scrutiny test to strike down diversity-based college-admissions programs. In *Hopwood v. Texas* (1996), the Fifth Circuit invalidated the race-based admissions process at the University of Texas School of Law. In *Johnson v. Board of Regents* (2001), a case in which I served as plaintiffs' counsel, the U.S. Court of Appeals of the 11th Circuit held that the University of Georgia's use of racial and gender preferences violated Titles VI and IX [of the 1964 Civil Rights Act]. The court held that a "point bonus for race" preference system was not narrowly tailored to advancing the university's professed interest in improving education, even if one assumed diversity was a compelling state interest.

Reduced to its essence, diversity is largely a semantical gloss used by academe to perpetuate minority admission quotas that had their genesis in old federal desegregation decrees used to integrate higher education after *Brown* [*v. Board of Education*, 1954]. Those draconian racial quotas were court-ordered, short-term agents of integration, designed to end segregation in education immediately. Diversity is the password coined by academe to allow these old racial quotas to slip past their court-ordered deadlines for termination and find permanency in the amorphous and all-encompassing concept of affirmative action.

Constitutional Analysis More Important than Diversity

We must not allow the aspirational nobility that rings out from lofty words like "diversity" to cloud the constitutional analysis. Diversity in academe-speak defies any concrete definition. Indeed, diversity works more like a religion than a constitutional principle. Its churches are our elite colleges, each a slightly different denomination of the faith. Its high priests are those in academe who profess to know what racial mix conjures up the best education.

True believers in diversity hold the heartfelt conviction that, from the original sin of discrimination, comes the greater good of an educational experience that theoretically moves certain subjectively designated races that "need help" into the mainstream American economy faster than would otherwise be the case.

There is no principled legal explanation as to why this kind of diversity, divorced from any remedial purpose, is not just a poorly disguised set-aside program, as pernicious in effect on those being discriminated against as any intentional act of bigotry. That does not seem to matter to the flock. Secure in the fact they have claimed the higher moral ground in their quest for racial fairness, the high priests confidently point to *Bakke* as the Bible that pronounces them correct both in their purpose and the discriminatory practices used to achieve it.

But equal protection, as an individual civil right, is imploded when you elevate diversity to a compelling state interest. Diversity is not limited by the usually mandatory requirement that the use of race must always be temporary and narrowly tailored to achieve a specific remedial purpose. The importance of that limitation is inescapable: Once the remedy is achieved, the discrimination and its measurable vestiges presumably go away, and there is no constitutional justification for continuing to discriminate.

No End to Diversity-Driven Quota System

By way of amicus brief, President [George W.] Bush has made the compelling point that diversity, Michigan style, constitutes an endless affirmative-action program designed to fill a quota that the university euphemistically calls a "critical mass." In *Grutter,* the Sixth Circuit specifically freed diversity from any temporal limitations with the incredible statement that "an interest in academic diversity does not have a self-contained stopping point." Even Justice Powell strongly disagreed with the proposition that racial discrimination that furthers the diversity factor should enjoy eternal life. . . .

Diversity, when constitutionally concocted, must be a far more subtle and varied blend of an applicant's past experiences, unique talents, challenges overcome, and personal qualities than that race-centric recipe. Surely, any fair surrogate for, or adjunct to, precisely measurable academic qualifications would have to be based on more than just skin color. Justice Powell acknowledged as much in *Bakke* when he opined that "the diversity that furthers a compelling state interest encompasses a far broader array of qualifications and characteristics of which racial . . . origin is but a single though important element."

The better approach is to award bonus points on a race-neutral basis to level the playing field for any truly deserving student whose lower grade-point averages and SAT scores correlate to overcoming poverty, a single-parent household, lack of English-language background, enrollment at an underperforming high school, a physical handicap, or an undiagnosed or untreated learning disability. That approach would provide a principled, nonracial justification for the clear favoritism shown such applicants, even though most beneficiaries would probably be minority applicants. But the Michigan admissions process does not work that way.

If you truly accept the great promise of *Brown* that government-sponsored racial discrimination will never again be allowed a role in the allocation of life-changing opportunities like education, then you must accept the undeniable fact that this promise does not depend on the skin color of the student.

White Applicants Denied Opportunities

No one denies that Jennifer Gratz, Barbara Grutter, and count-less other qualified white applicants have been denied invalu-able educational opportunities by Michigan because of their skin color. Their failure to gain admission is attributable, like Allan Bakke's, to the improbable sin of living "a storybook life of middle class virtue," as J. Harvie Wilkinson III, the chief judge of the U.S. Court of Appeals for the Fourth Circuit, put it in *From Brown to Bakke*. No amount of "robust exchange of ideas" [*Bakke*] can justify that outcome under the 14th Amendment.

The most interesting and important law cases, to lawyers and laymen alike, tend to turn on constitutional issues. The most compelling of that genre are those precedent-setting de-cisions that prohibit widespread and generally accepted state-sponsored practices because they, despite all good intentions, violate an individual citizen's constitutional rights. There is something quintessentially American about such outcomes where one person, armed only with the power of the spoken and written word emanating from the Bill of Rights, stops an entire government dead in its tracks.

That is what young Gratz and Grutter intend to do, and we will be a better nation if they succeed. It is the victories of individual citizens, both large and small, in these defining kinds of cases that blend together to form a veneer over our individual civil rights called precedent that hardens with every reaffirmation, and protects us all from errant legislation, mis-guided state policy or practice, and even from rogue judges who would substitute their ideas about what is "good" for this country for the collective wisdom of the Founding Fathers.

In the final analysis, diversity is nothing more than a con-stitutional unicorn, born of the myth that sprang from the musings of a single justice in the cacophony we call *Bakke*. One has been seen roaming the campus at Ann Arbor [the University of Michigan], and it now falls to the Supreme Court to declare it the fable that we know it to be.

> *"For those bent on racial preference,*
> *the 'winks, nods, and disguises' [of*
> *race-based college admissions pro-*
> *grams] . . . have now . . . been made*
> *a practical necessity."*

Grutter Will Lead to Disguised Racial Discrimination

Carl Cohen

In rendering their decision in Grutter v. Bollinger, *the Supreme Court justices had to consider the 1978* Regents of the University of California v. Bakke *case. In the* Bakke *ruling a splintered Court decided that some consideration could be given to race in admissions to universities and professional schools, but any sort of quotas, racial balancing, or point system was unconstitutional. These kinds of policies failed "strict scrutiny," the legal principle that all classifications based on race were suspected of being unconstitutional unless they had very limited goals.*

In the following excerpt University of Michigan philosophy professor Carl Cohen holds that with Grutter *the Supreme Court has now made "diversity" a compelling state interest. Although they are forbidden to use point systems or quotas, institutions will now be free to use "individualized" or "holistic" treatment of admissions files in order to achieve a desired level of minority admissions. Cohen concludes that the vagueness of the ruling will lead to the creation of admissions policies that conform to the* Grutter *ruling but, in practice, seek proportional representa-*

Carl Cohen, "Winks, Nods, Disguises—and Racial Preference," *Commentary,* September 2003. Copyright © 2003 by the American Jewish Committee. All rights reserved. Reproduced by permission of the publisher and the author.

tion of minority students. As such, he argues, they will violate the Constitution's equal-protection clause.

I n *Gratz v. Bollinger,* the Supreme Court of the United States [held] . . . that the numerical admissions system used by Michigan's undergraduate college, in which a given number of points was awarded to all applicants in certain ethnic categories, violated the equal-protection clause of the Fourteenth Amendment as well as the Civil Rights Act of 1964. But on the same day, in *Grutter v. Bollinger,* the Court held that "the educational benefits that flow from a diverse student body" were indeed, in the context of higher education, a compelling state interest. Moreover, the particular form of deliberate racial discrimination practiced by the law school of the University of Michigan was found to be consistent with the constitutional guarantee of equal protection of the laws.

Bitter Dissent

The diversity principle, even if only in one context, and with heavy restrictions, has thus been embedded in law. . . . In the meantime, in the tension between these two latest decisions, what was muddy in *Bakke* has become muddier still.

Much damage has been inflicted on the standard of strict scrutiny itself. As the four dissenting opinions in *Grutter* (the law-school decision) make vividly, even bitterly, clear, the need of the state of Michigan for diversity of skin colors in its university admissions was hardly "compelling." Even the maintenance of a law school by the state of Michigan, as Justice Clarence Thomas pointed out, although surely a good thing, is not a compelling need; many states thrive without one. Nor, for that matter, has the university's program delivered on its promise: exhaustive research has shown that its purported benefits (i.e., the promotion of tolerance and understanding for the views of "diverse" others) have been in scant evidence. No genuinely "compelling" educational need is being served.

As for the second prong of the standard of strict scrutiny—the requirement that, even if some compelling state need has been identified, the use of racial classifications must be narrowly tailored to the fulfillment of that need—the race preferences given by the law school, no less than the rejected admissions system of Michigan's undergraduate college, likewise failed to satisfy it. Demonstrating this failure formed the nub of Chief Justice [William] Rehnquist's dissenting opinion in *Grutter,* in which he was joined by Justices Clarence Thomas, Antonin Scalia, and Anthony Kennedy. It has not been widely understood.

According to the University of Michigan, the educational benefits of diversity were said to flow from the creation of a "critical mass" of minority representatives in the student body: a number sufficiently large that the members of a given minority in a given class would not feel themselves "isolated" in that class. The racial instrument used in law-school admissions was, the university held, narrowly tailored to this end. Unlike the practice in the undergraduate college, the law school, in evaluating applicants, claimed not to rely on some fixed numerical value mechanically awarded to every member of certain ethnic groups. Instead, the critical masses needed for the three designated minorities—African-Americans, Native Americans, and Hispanics—were said to have been artfully assembled through the use of highly sensitive reviews of each individual applicant.

Indeed, in the earlier, district-court trial of *Grutter,* as in the university's written arguments for the Supreme Court, the law school had gone to great lengths to avoid any mention whatsoever of numbers or percentages. And for good reason: any open confession of this kind would have exposed the school to the same condemnation received by the undergraduate college in *Gratz.* But the entire law-school system was a deception. The dissenting opinion of the Chief Justice proved this.

A Question of "Critical Mass"

In any given class of students, a "critical mass," whatever it is, cannot be greatly different in size for African-Americans from what it is for other minorities; nor can it differ greatly in one year from what it was three years earlier, at least if the class itself has not changed in size. In fact, however, the numbers of the several minorities admitted to the Michigan law school in order to form their respective "critical masses" differed very greatly from minority to minority and, for each minority, from year to year. Calling attention to this starkly revealing feature of the school's admissions over a period of many years, and inserting numerical tables into his opinion to render the matter incontrovertible, Justice Rehnquist showed that the number of those admitted in each minority closely tracked the number of applications by members of that minority.

The figures themselves are worth examining. In recent years, the Michigan law school has offered admission each year, on average, to sixteen Native Americans, 51 Hispanics, and 100 African-Americans. If what had really been sought was a critical mass of each minority—that is, a number sufficiently large to ward off feelings of isolation within the class—and if the yield of 50 offers was enough to achieve that in the case of Hispanics, it cannot be the case (as the Chief Justice pointed out) that the yield of 100 offers was needed among some other minority, or that the yield of sixteen offers would be sufficient in the case of still another.

How did the numbers themselves come about? Rehnquist described the process. When, in 1995, 9.7 percent of the applicant pool was African-American, 9.4 percent of those admitted were African-Americans. Five years later, when 7.5 percent of the applicant pool was African-American, 7.3 percent of those admitted were African-Americans. A similar pattern was manifest throughout.

This "tight correlation between the percentage of applicants and admittees of a given race," Rehnquist wrote, devastatingly, could

> only be the result of very careful race-based planning. . . .
> We are bound to conclude that the law school has managed its admission program, not to achieve a "critical mass," but to extend offers of admission to members of selected minority groups in proportion to their statistical representation in the applicant pool.

Despite the law school's repeated protestations to the contrary, the statistics demonstrate that it was seeking some proportional representation of minorities in its entering classes. Its real objective was not critical mass—this, in Rehnquist's words, was "simply a sham"—but racial balance. But it could not have proclaimed this obvious truth, contending forthrightly that such proportionality would serve as its achievement of "diversity," for the simple reason that the admission of persons simply to achieve certain percentages of various ethnic groups is "patently unconstitutional." Justice Powell had made that point crisply in *Bakke* decades ago, and the same proposition was affirmed by the majority in *Grutter* without reservation. Instead, the law school engaged in a sham. . . .

Race-Based Admissions Policies Will Spread Nationwide

Thanks to the Court's decision, still worse is now to come. The law-school system, a sham in reality, has been elevated to the status of a model—and not only for law schools. As we have seen, Michigan's use of race in undergraduate admissions, which did not pretend to be "individualized" or "holistic," was on that account found to be flatly unconstitutional. But henceforth, Michigan and many other universities will formulate their undergraduate preferential schemes in phrases echoing the language of the law-school program. Beginning now, "individualized review," "holistic," "critical mass," "plus factor," "a particular applicant's file," and the like will appear ubiquitously and talismanically in the description of admission systems from coast to coast.

Of course, it will be far easier to profess such highly individualized review systems than to realize them. And so a second-level sham will be explicitly invited: a fraud imitating a fraud.

Consider: the law school at Michigan enrolls some 350 new students each year. Of the several thousand who apply, a good number are speedily disqualified, with many of the remaining applicants interviewed in person and the complete file of every admitted applicant examined by a single person, the assistant dean for admissions. Even though, at the Michigan law school, the real goal has been racial balancing, the requisite process of "individualization," as approved by the Court, is conceivably doable, if with some strain.

The undergraduate college at Michigan is a rather different affair. It receives more than 25,000 applications for admission each year. Picture a gymnasium in which those fat application files are stacked in piles six feet high; there will be some 350 of these piles, or more, pretty nearly stuffing the gymnasium to the gills. Now imagine that each application is to be evaluated comparatively, with race and many other factors given varying and appropriate weights in the assessment of each candidate. Remember, no numerical value for ethnicity is to be assigned, no quantitative system applied.

An Impractical Policy

How, in the name of reason, is the comparison of these 25,000 applicants to be carried out? Even for an army of admissions officers, the exercise would be hopeless. It is utterly impossible for the University of Michigan—not to speak of universities in

Minnesota and Ohio and other states where undergraduate colleges are substantially larger still—to review all the particular qualifications of each of tens of thousands of applicants, weighing race as but one factor, without using some numerical calculus. Any future claim to that effect is guaranteed to be a deception.

In its written argument defending the mechanical award of points for race in undergraduate admissions, the University of Michigan granted candidly that "the volume of applications and the presentation of applicant information make it impractical for [the undergraduate college] to use the . . . admissions system" of the law school. Of course. That is why the university argued, in effect, that since the racial results it sought could only be achieved using a system of numerical weights, such a system must be permissible, for there is no other way to achieve the approved aim of diversity.

No! responded the Court in *Gratz*. The use of race is permitted in some ways, but it is not urged, and you are certainly not entitled to do whatever you think is required. The Court's strictures were not to be bypassed: a university may not "employ whatever means it desires to achieve the stated goal of diversity without regard to the limits imposed by our strict-scrutiny analysis." Nor did "the fact that the implementation of a program providing individualized consideration might present administrative challenges . . . render constitutional an otherwise problematic system." So, under *Gratz*, the university has been forbidden to do what it asserts it must do in order to achieve the racial objective it asserts it must pursue and which, under *Grutter*, has now been found "compelling." Here, in the pull of the two decisions against each other, is indeed a recipe for still more pervasive obfuscation and more shameful hypocrisy.

Camouflaging Racial Preferences

Justice Ruth [Bader] Ginsburg, who dissented from the majority in *Gratz*, saw this clearly. Writing in support of the now-unlawful point system, she frankly acknowledged that universities have already been deceitful and sly in this arena, resorting to "camouflage" by encouraging minority applicants and their supporters to convey their ethnic identification deviously and backhandedly in personal essays and letters of recommendation. Justice Ginsburg then concluded: "If honesty is the best policy, surely Michigan's accurately described, fully disclosed college affirmative-action program is preferable to achieving similar numbers through winks, nods, and disguises." Narrow tailoring need not be faked; instead, in Ginsburg's view, it could simply be ignored. A non-individualized program, assigning a fixed number of points for skin color, was the answer. Unless we permitted it, the result would be widespread cheating.

She was certainly right about the cheating. But cheating is already endemic, and is now bound to spread further. For those bent on racial preference, the "winks, nods, and disguises" decried by Ginsburg have now, thanks to her and her likeminded colleagues in *Grutter*, been made a practical necessity.

In a footnote to the opinion striking down the undergraduate point system, Chief Justice Rehnquist called Ginsburg's observations "remarkable," and answered them sharply: First, they suggest that universities—to whose academic judgment we are told in *Grutter* we should defer—will pursue their affirmative-action programs whether or not they violate the United States Constitution. Second, they recommend that these violations should be dealt with, not by requiring the universities to obey the Constitution, but by changing the Constitution so that it conforms to the conduct of the universities. . . .

Voters Will Decide the Issue

But the controversy will also move from the courtroom to the ballot box. If the Supreme Court has found that, in the interest of diversity, race preference may be given, it remains for the people of the several states to decide for themselves whether, in their state, race preference is to be forbidden. In Michigan, for example, every effort will be made by the time of the presidential election of 2004 to place on the ballot a Michigan Civil Rights Initiative—an equivalent of California's Proposition 209. The operative sentence in that proposition, now incorporated in the California constitution, is nearly identical to a critical passage of the Civil Rights Act of 1964, with the addition of five words that appear here in emphasis. It reads:

> The state shall not discriminate against, *or grant preferential treatment to,* any individual or group on the basis of race, sex, color, ethnicity, or national origin in the operation of public employment, public education, or public contracting.

Once the matter is on the ballot, it will also become more difficult for legislators and political candidates to dodge this controversy as they have so often done in the past. Will they urge their constituents to vote against a proposition forbidding race preference? If so, must we not conclude that they support race preference?

The decision of the U.S. Supreme Court in *Grutter v. Bollinger* is disheartening in the extreme. But the governing rule in this matter will come ultimately from the citizenry, and we must trust that the large majority of Americans, as reported in survey after survey and confirmed in election after election, continues to find racism of every sort disgusting. I was wrong about the outcome of the battle in court; now the war must move to other fronts.

"[Grutter] is a strong, positive step forward—a real cause for celebration."

Grutter Will Lead to Increased Opportunities for Minorities

William G. Bowen

William G. Bowen is president of the Andrew W. Mellon Foundation, a nonprofit organization that conducts research into education issues. He served as president of Princeton University from 1972 to 1988. He is the author of twenty books, including The Shape of the River: Long-Term Consequences of Considering Race in College and University Admissions.

In the following excerpt from a 2004 article, Bowen celebrates the decision of the Supreme Court in Grutter v. Bollinger. *Rather than eliminating all forms of racial preferences in university and professional school admissions, as some had feared, the Court's decision strengthened the case for diversity. The opinion cites the need for diversity not only to improve educational outcomes but also to enhance the legitimacy of America's leaders. If some ethnic groups do not have access to the training grounds for such leaders, including top law schools such as the University of Michigan, then those ethnic groups will not be represented among the nation's business, educational, political, and military elites. Bowen insists that such representation is necessary for the United States to remain a healthy society. The* Grutter *decision will make this outcome more likely.*

William G. Bowen, "*Grutter* : Where Do We Go from Here?" *Journal of Blacks in Higher Education,* Summer 2004. Copyright © 2004 by CH II Publishers, Inc. Reproduced by permission of the author.

The legislative challenges to race-sensitive admissions policies in California and Washington, and the challenge posed by the *Hopwood* [*v. Texas*] case in Texas, all pale in comparison to the importance of the two University of Michigan cases heard by the U.S. Supreme Court last year [2003]. Before the decision, Charles Vest, president of MIT [The Massachusetts Institute of Technology], saw all that has been accomplished, and all that can be accomplished in the future, as "hanging by a thread." Vest's concern, shared by many others, was that the "thread" represented by Justice [Lewis] Powell's seemingly innocuous phrase in [*Regents of the University of California v.*] *Bakke* justifying the use of race "as one of many factors" in making admissions decisions could be severed by "one snip of the judicial scissors." The clear goal of the plaintiffs in the Michigan cases, and their backers, was to eliminate altogether the freedom of colleges and universities to consider race in deciding who to admit.

Dodging a Bullet

Avoiding a flat prohibition on consideration of race, then, was the bullet to be dodged—and it was dodged, to the immense relief of the higher education community and legions of others who believe strongly, often passionately, in the importance of continuing to take race into account. The central message of the majority opinion in *Grutter* (the law school case) was summarized well by *New York Times* reporter Linda Greenhouse:

> The result of today's rulings was that Justice Powell's solitary view that there was a "compelling state interest" in racial diversity, a position that had appeared undermined by the Court's subsequent equal protection rulings in other contexts and that some lower federal courts had boldly repudiated, has now been endorsed by five justices and placed on a stronger footing than ever before.

The Court's opinion, as Justice [Sandra Day] O'Connor delivered it, is unequivocal:

> Today, we hold that the Law School has a compelling interest in attaining a diverse student body.... The Equal Protection Clause does not prohibit the Law School's narrowly tailored use of race in admissions decisions to further a compelling interest in obtaining the educational benefits that flow from a diverse student body.

The *Grutter* case without question strengthened President Vest's "thread" (turned it into a "rope," as it were). It did this, first, by replacing a "fractured," "splintered" decision in *Bakke* with a solid five-justice opinion supporting diversity as a compelling state interest. In addition, the Court expanded dramatically the rationale for enrolling a diverse class to include not only the on-campus educational benefits of diversity but also the preparation of larger numbers of well-educated minority candidates for leadership positions in the professions, business, academia, the military, and government—a second principal objective of race-sensitive admissions which the evidence demonstrates has been achieved. Many of us have long regarded Justice Powell's sole focus on learning outcomes as too narrow, and too limited a justification for race-sensitive admissions policies. In now embracing both the improvement in learning outcomes and the preparation of more minority students for important roles in national life as components of a "compelling state interest" in racial diversity, the Court has aligned its reasoning with the thinking and stated missions of almost all of American higher education.

A Positive Step Forward

This is why *Grutter* is much more than "bullet-dodging"; it is a strong, positive step forward—a real cause for celebration. This decision is also of fundamental importance for a more general reason: it rebuts the idea that the Court understands the Fourteenth Amendment as endorsing only the "anticlassification" principle (that "government may not classify on the basis of race"). Fortunately, the "antisubordination" principle ("the conviction that it is wrong for the state to engage in practices that enforce the inferior social status of historically oppressed peoples") is alive and well, much as the Court disguise[s] its endorsement of it.

This conclusion is gratifying in and of itself. It is also encouraging to see the numerous references in the Court's opinion to the role played by social science research in bolstering the arguments for this conclusion, the obviously important role played by amici briefs, and the eloquence with which the Court argues its position. In *Grutter*, the Court refers to briefs submitted on behalf of American businesses "making clear that the skills needed in today's increasing global marketplace can only be developed through exposure to widely diverse people, cultures, ideas, and viewpoints. . . . What is more, highranking retired officers and civilian leaders of the United States military assert that, 'based on [their] decades of experience,' a 'highly qualified, racially diverse officer corps . . . is essential to the military's ability to fulfill its principal mission to provide national security.'"

The Court then takes a still broader tack, which hearkens back to sentiments expressed by [Thomas] Jefferson. "This Court has long recognized that 'education . . . is the very foundation of good citizenship.' . . . For this reason, the diffusion of knowledge and opportunity through public institutions of higher education must be accessible to all individuals regardless of race or ethnicity. . . . Effective participation by members of all racial and ethnic groups in the civil life of our Nation is essential if the dream of one Nation, indivisible, is to be realized." After next emphasizing the particular importance of law schools as training grounds for a larger number of our Nation's leaders, the Court observes: "In order to cultivate a set of leaders with legitimacy in the eyes of the citizenry, it is necessary that the path to leadership be visibly open to talented and qualified individuals of every race and ethnicity." These stirring words introduce the concept of "democratic legitimacy" as one of the principal societal needs that race-sensitive admissions addresses.

Another important part of the O'Connor opinion is its rejection of the claim that "race-neutral means exist to obtain the educational benefits of student body diversity that the Law School seeks." The opinion says flatly: "We disagree. Narrow tailoring does not require exhaustion of every conceivable race-neutral alternative." What it does require is "serious, good faith consideration of workable race-neutral alternatives that will achieve the diversity the university seeks." The Court is dismissive of ideas such as using a lottery system, lowering admissions standards for all students, and adopting "percentage plans" such as the one in use in Texas (whereby all high school students above a certain class-rank threshold are automatically guaranteed admission to the University of Texas). . . .

Risks of More Litigation

One large question is whether the decisions reached in the University of Michigan cases will "stabilize" this area of the law, at least for a time, or whether they will provoke other suits. Justice [Antonin] Scalia, in his dissenting opinion, seemed almost to invite more challenges:

> Today's split double header [the opposite decisions in the *Grutter* and *Gratz* cases] seems perversely designed to prolong the controversy and the litigation. Some future lawsuits will presumably focus on whether the discriminatory scheme in question contains enough evaluation of the applicant "as an individual.". . . Still other suits may challenge the bona fides of the institution's expressed commitment to the educational benefits of diversity that immunize the discriminatory scheme in *Grutter*. (Tempting targets, one would suppose, will be those universities that talk the talk of multiculturalism and racial diversity in the courts but walk

the walk of tribalism and racial segregation on their campuses. . .) And still other suits may claim that the institution's racial preferences have gone below or above the mystical *Grutter*-approved "critical mass."

It seems clear that in crafting their admissions policies, colleges and universities will need to follow closely the quite clear guidance provided in *Grutter*, and I presume that the overwhelming majority will do so—in fact, most conform today. Also, I agree with Justice Scalia that those in higher education who have been (properly) extolling the virtues of "cross-racial understanding" and "learning through diversity" should align practices with educational philosophies in all facets of college and university life.

An Establishment Consensus

Organizations like the Center for Individual Rights (CIR) and the Center for Equal Opportunity will surely challenge institutions which they believe are near, if not over, the edge of compliance with applicable law. But there are also new political (as well as judicial) realities for these groups to contemplate. Without question, the extraordinarily strong support for race-sensitive admissions reflected in the outpouring of briefs on Michigan's behalf is a factor to be weighed by all parties to these debates. It is more than mildly ironic that in stimulating and supporting the *Grutter* and *Gratz* challenges, the anti-affirmative action groups managed to provoke the creation of a broad-based alliance among businesses, labor unions, religious groups, professional and scholarly associations, the military, and a wide range of academics that created something approaching a societal consensus (within the "establishment," at least) in favor of taking race into account in admissions decisions. The breadth and depth of support was truly amazing to behold.

Debate continues among lawyers and within the higher education community as to whether race-targeted financial aid awards will be permissible in the aftermath of *Grutter-Gratz*. (One irony is that Pepperdine University, with its strong ties to the conservative and evangelical movements, is nonetheless battling with anti-affirmative action groups to retain its minority-only scholarship program.) Similarly, there is uncertainty as to what colleges and universities can and cannot do in efforts to recruit and promote a more diverse faculty. These are large questions, different in some important respects from the admissions and "enrichment" questions; they are not as simple as they may at first seem to be, but there is no time today to do more than single them out as deserving further study and reflection. I am skeptical, however, that there will be many, if any, settings in which race exclusivity is going to be permitted.

The "open question" that has received the most attention, and is the most challenging, has to do with the permissible duration of race-sensitive admissions policies. Was O'Connor's widely quoted 25-year comment ("We expect that 25 years from now, the use of racial preferences will no longer be necessary to further the interest approved today") merely a hopeful prediction (estimate), or was it meant to impose a binding limit? There is no way of being sure. Nonetheless, it would certainly seem prudent to treat the 25-year limit as presumptively binding. Both [Harvard law professor] Derek Bok and [economist] Glenn Loury have described this part of the Court's decision as a "wake-up call," and those of us interested in closing racial gaps of all kinds should certainly want to help create—as quickly as possible—conditions in which racial preferences in admissions are unnecessary.

Practical Possibilities

But however desirable it may be to meet the 25-year goal, is this possible from a practical perspective? The basic reason why racial preferences are needed at present is that underrepresented minorities do significantly less well on traditional measures of college preparation (especially test scores) than do whites and Asians. Can the preparation gap be eliminated over the next 25 years? The sizes of the current gap tells us that this is a daunting task. For example, on national reading tests, only 16 percent of African Americans and 22 percent of Hispanics reached the "proficient" level or higher, compared to 34 percent of Asian Americans and 42 percent of whites. Moreover, the factors responsible for such differences are so deep-seated that any reasonable person has to be skeptical that there are quick fixes.

At the same time, there is evidence that black-white gaps in both income and test scores have been converging. But will they converge fast enough? Projections provide one basis for forming at least a rough judgment as to what the future holds—even as we recognize that projecting any trends out over 25 years is a hazardous undertaking. Professors Alan Krueger, Jesse Rothstein, and Sarah Turner are in the early stages of simulating the likely effects of these "convergence" trends on black-white gaps in preparedness over the next quarter century, and their initial (highly preliminary) results indicate that eliminating the need for race-sensitive admissions over this period will be a very challenging task. . . .

What are we to conclude? There is no reason to believe that the need for race-sensitive admissions will end within the next 25 years simply as a result of trends and policies already in place. If 25 years is a hard limit, it might benefit from some more analysis. The goal is laudable and we can certainly anticipate some progress. But elimination of the need for racial preferences will not "just happen."

Organizations to Contact

American Civil Liberties Union (ACLU)
125 Broad St., 18th Fl.
New York, NY 10004
(212) 549-2500
e-mail: aclu@aclu.org
Web site: www.aclu.org

The ACLU is a national organization that works to defend the rights guaranteed by the U.S. Constitution. Its primary work is to support court cases against government actions that violate these rights. The ACLU also publishes and distributes policy statements, pamphlets, and the semiannual newsletter *Civil Liberties Alert.*

Anti-Defamation League (ADL)
823 United Nations Plaza
New York, NY 10017
(212) 490-2525
Web site: www.adl.org

ADL works to stop the defamation of Jews and to ensure fair treatment for all U.S. citizens. It publishes numerous reports addressing specific issues such as hate crimes, white supremacist groups, and Islamic terrorism.

Cato Institute
1000 Massachusetts Ave. NW
Washington, DC 20001-5403
(202) 842-0200 • fax: (202) 842-3490
Web site: www.cato.org

The Cato Institute is a libertarian public policy research foundation dedicated to limiting the role of government and protecting individual liberties. It researches claims of discrimination and opposes affirmative action. The institute publishes the quarterly magazine *Regulation*, the bimonthly *Cato Policy Report*, and numerous books.

Center for Equal Opportunity (CEO)
14 Pidgeon Hill Dr., Suite 500
  Sterling, VA 20165
(703) 421-5443 • fax: (703) 421-6401
Web site: www.ceousa.org

Generally considered conservative and anti–affirmative action, the Center for Equal Opportunity is headed by former Reagan administration official Linda Chavez. CEO focuses on three policy areas in particular: racial preferences, immigration and assimilation, and multicultural education.

Center for the Study of Popular Culture (CSPC)
4401 Wilshire Dr., 4th Fl.
  Los Angeles, CA 90010
(323) 556-2550
e-mail: info@cspc.org
Web site: www.cspc.org

CSPC is a conservative educational organization that addresses topics such as political correctness, cultural diversity, and discrimination. Its civil rights project promotes equal opportunity for all individuals and provides legal assistance to citizens challenging affirmative action. The center publishes four magazines: *Heterodoxy, Defender, Report Card,* and *COMINT.*

Citizens' Commission on Civil Rights (CCCR)
2000 M St. NW, Suite 400
Washington, DC 20036
(202) 659-5565 • fax: (202) 223-5302
e-mail: citizens@cccr.org
Web site: www.cccr.org

CCCR monitors the federal government's enforcement of antidiscrimination laws and promotes equal opportunity for all. It publishes reports on affirmative action and desegregation as well as the book *One Nation Indivisible: The Civil Rights Challenge for the 1990s.*

The Heritage Foundation
214 Massachusetts Ave. NE
  Washington, DC 20002-4999
(202) 546-4400 • fax: (202) 546-8328

e-mail: info@heritage.org
Web site: www.heritage.org

A long-established conservative public policy research institute, the Heritage Foundation generally opposes affirmative action. Its reports and other publications typically recommend private sector solutions to address discrimination against women and minorities. In addition to books and special reports, Heritage publishes the quarterly journal *Policy Review* and the bimonthly newsletter *Heritage Today.*

Mexican American Legal Defense and Education Fund (MALDEF)
MALDEF National Headquarters
Los Angeles, CA 90014
(213) 629-2512
Web site: www.maldef.org

MALDEF was founded in 1968 in order to promote the rights of Mexican Americans and Mexicans in the United States. The organization sponsors legal actions against laws it considers discriminatory toward Mexican Americans and other minorities. It promotes affirmative action and also focuses on educational efforts.

National Association for the Advancement of Colored People (NAACP)
4805 Mt. Hope Dr., Baltimore, MD 21215-3297
(410) 580-5760 (education) • fax: (410) 580-5790 (legal)
e-mail (Washington, D.C., Bureau):
washingtonbureau@naacpnet.org
Web site:www.naacp.org

The NAACP is the oldest and largest civil rights organization in the United States. It advocates for the protection of the civil rights of African Americans and other minorities. It also sponsors educational programs devoted to developing future civil rights leaders. It publishes the magazine *Crisis* ten times a year as well as books, pamphlets, and newsletters.

United States Commission on Civil Rights
624 Ninth St. NW, Suite 500
  Washington, DC 20425
(202) 376-7700
Web site: www.usccr.gov

A fact-finding body, the commission reports directly to Congress and the president on the effectiveness of equal opportunity laws and programs. It also publishes reports on various aspects of civil rights. A catalog of these reports can be obtained from its Publication Management Division. In addition, many can be downloaded from the commission's Web site.

For Further Research

Books

Paul D. Buchanan, *Race Relations in the United States: A Chronology, 1896–2005*. Jefferson, NC: McFarland, 2005.

Lincoln Caplan, *Up Against the Law: Affirmative Action and the Supreme Court*. New York: Twentieth Century Fund, 1997.

Robert J. Cottrol, *Brown v. Board of Education: Caste, Culture, and the Constitution*. Lawrence: University Press of Kansas, 2003.

Alan M. Dershowitz, *America on Trial: Inside the Legal Battles That Transformed Our Nation*. New York: Warner, 2004.

Neal Devins and Davison M. Douglas, *A Year at the Supreme Court*. Durham, NC: Duke University Press, 2004.

Leon Friedman, *Brown v. Board: The Landmark Oral Argument Before the Supreme Court*. New York: New Press, 2004.

Katharine Gelber, *Speaking Back: The Free Speech Versus Hate Speech Debate*. Philadelphia: John Benjamins, 2002.

Annette Gordon-Reed, *Race on Trial: Law and Justice in American History*. New York: Oxford University Press, 2002.

Jon B. Gould, *Speak No Evil: The Triumph of Hate Speech Regulation*. Chicago: University of Chicago Press, 2005.

Maureen Harrison and Steve Gilbert, *Landmark Decisions of the United States Supreme Court*. Beverly Hills, CA: Excellent Books, 1991.

Thomas R. Hensley, *The Boundaries of Freedom of Expression and Order in American Democracy*. Kent, OH: Kent State University Press, 2001.

Peter H. Irons, *Jim Crow's Children: The Broken Promise of the Brown Decision*. New York: Viking, 2002.

Charles A. Lofgren, *The Plessy Case: A Legal-Historical Interpretation*. New York: Oxford University Press, 1987.

Waldo E. Martin, *Brown v. Board of Education: A Brief History with Documents*. Boston: St. Martin's, 1998.

Otto H. Olsen, *The Thin Disguise: Turning Point in Negro History; Plessy v. Ferguson; a Documentary Presentation, 1864–1896*. New York: Humanities, 1967.

Michael J. Perry, *We the People: The Fourteenth Amendment and the Supreme Court*. New York: Oxford University Press, 1999.

Clarke Rountree, *Brown v. Board of Education at Fifty: A Rhetorical Perspective*. Lanham, MD: Lexington, 2004.

Bernard Schwartz, *Behind Bakke: Affirmative Action and the Supreme Court*. New York: New York University Press, 1988.

Timothy C. Shiell, *Campus Hate Speech on Trial*. Lawrence: University Press of Kansas, 1998.

L.W. Sumner, *The Hateful and the Obscene: Studies in the Limits of Free Expression*. Toronto: University of Toronto Press, 2004.

Brook Thomas, *Plessy v. Ferguson: A Brief History with Documents*. Boston: Bedford, 1997.

Alexander Tsesis, *Destructive Messages: How Hate Speech Paves the Way for Harmful Social Movements*. New York: New York University Press 2002.

Melvin I. Urofsky, *A Conflict of Rights: The Supreme Court and Affirmative Action*. New York: Collier Macmillan, 1991.

Mark Stuart Weiner, *Black Trials: Citizenship from the Beginnings of Slavery to the End of Caste*. New York: Alfred A. Knopf, 2004.

Robert Zelnick, *Swing Dance: Justice O'Connor and the Michigan Muddle.* Stanford, CA: Hoover Institution, 2004.

Periodicals

Janus Adams, "48 Years After 'Brown,' Civil Rights Erode," *USA Today,* May 17, 2002.

Elizabeth S. Anderson, "Racial Integration as a Compelling Interest," *Constitutional Commentary,* Spring 2004.

Fred Beauford, "Affirmative Action: 40th Anniversary," *Black Issues Book Review,* September/October 2005.

Black Issues in Higher Education, "U.S. Supreme Court Debates Use of Racial Segregation in Prisons," December 2, 2004.

Sheryl Henderson Blunt, "Muzzled Speech," *Christianity Today,* March 2005.

William G. Bowen, "*Grutter* : Where Do We Go from Here?" *Journal of Blacks in Higher Education,* Summer 2004.

Thandeka Chapman, "Peddling Backwards: Reflections of *Plessy* and *Brown* in the Rockford Public Schools De Jure Desegregation Efforts," *Race, Ethnicity & Education,* March 2005.

Christian Century, "Still Separate and Unequal," October 4, 2005.

N. Lee Cooper, "The Harlan Standard," *Journal of the American Bar Association,* June 1997.

Richard Delgado, "Hate Cannot Be Tolerated," *USA Today,* March 3, 2004.

Debra J. Dickerson, "The Great White Way," *Mother Jones,* September/October 2005.

Mary C. Doyle, "From Desegregation to Resegregation: Public Schools in Norfolk, Virginia 1954–2002," *Journal of African American History,* Winter/Spring 2005.

R.F. Drinan, "Should Hate Speech on Campus Be Punished?" *America*, September 21, 1991.

Myrlie Evers-Williams, "A Long Way to Go," *USA Today*, February 23, 2005.

Bay Fang, "A Woman with Strong Opinions," *U.S. News & World Report*, November 7, 2005.

Douglas J. Ficker, "From *Roberts* to *Plessy* : Educational Segregation and the 'Separate but Equal' Doctrine," *Journal of Negro History*, Fall 1999.

Hung-Gay Fung, "Stop the Racist Madness," *Chinese American Forum*, July 2005.

Linda Greenhouse, "Free Speech or Hate Speech? Court Weighs Cross Burning," *New York Times*, May 29, 2002.

Michael Greve, "Speech Impediments," *National Review*, October 10, 1994.

Frederick Hess, "The 'Critical Mass' Mess," *American Enterprise*, October 2003.

Jeffrey D. Hockett, "The Battle over *Brown*'s Legitimacy," *Journal of Supreme Court History*, January 2003.

Steven F. Lawson, "The Pursuit of Fairness: A History of Affirmative Action," *Journal of Southern History*, August 2005.

Jeffrey S. Lehman, "'Integration,' Not 'Diversity,'" *Chronicle of Higher Education*, April 23, 2004.

Alfonso López-Vasquez, "Affirmative Action in the Name of Restitution, Equity, Diversity, and Cultural Democracy," *Diverse: Issues in Higher Education*, September 22, 2005.

Richard Magat, "Nearly Forgotten," *Commonweal*, February 11, 2005.

Judith Lynne McConnell and Blythe F. Hinitz, "In Their Words: A Living History of the *Brown* Decision," *Educational Studies*, February 2005.

Kate O'Beirne, "Set-Aside Set-To," *National Review*, November 11, 2005.

Robert S. Pecke and Charles F. Williams, "Hate Crimes," *Journal of the American Bar Association*, May 1993.

David Lewis Schaefer, "Affirmative Action Around the World: An Empirical Study," *Society*, September/October 2005.

Noam Scheiber, "Racial Justice," *New Republic*, August 2005.

Peter Schmidt and Anne K. Walters, "Michigan's Affirmative-Action Battle Is Not Over Yet," *Chronicle of Higher Education*, November 11, 2005.

Girardeau A. Spann, "The Dark Side of *Grutter*," *Constitutional Commentary*, Spring 2004.

Abigail Thernstrom and Stephan Thernstrom, "Have We Overcome?" *Commentary*, November 2004.

Richard R. Valencia, "The Mexican American Struggle for Equal Educational Opportunity in *Mendez v. Westminster*: Helping to Pave the Way for *Brown v. Board of Education*," *Teachers College Record*, March 2005.

Amy Stuart Wells and Lamar P. Miller, "*Brown v. Board of Education* at 50: Looking Back While Moving Forward: An Introduction," *Teachers College Record*, March 2005.

Web Sites

American Civil Rights Institute (www.acri.org). This Web site was founded by Ward Connerly, a major opponent of affirmative action in education. The site has links to the friend-of-the-court briefs that the institute has filed in various cases as well as the text of the California Civil Rights Initiative, the ballot proposition that outlawed affirmative action in California college admissions.

Brown Foundation for Educational Equity, Excellence and Research (http://brownvboard.org). This Web site contains an exhibit detailing the history of African American education. Pages give information on blacks in education from before the Revolutionary War to the present. It also offers a useful "Myths vs. Facts About *Brown v. Board*" page.

Brown v. Board of Education National Historic Site (www.nps.gov/brvb). Web site of the National Historic Site that celebrates *Brown v. Board*. The site provides useful summaries of many of the desegregation cases leading up to or concurrent with *Brown v. Board of Education*.

Legal Information Institute at Cornell University Law School/ Supreme Court Decisions by Topic (http:// supct.law.cornell.edu/supct/cases/topic.htm). This Web page, part of a large archive of court decisions hosted by Cornell University Law School, enables users to find court cases quickly by topic. Discrimination and segregation are included in the topic list.

Modern Civil Rights Movement Timeline (www.as.ua.edu/ history/204note3.htm). Hosted by the University of Alabama history department, this Web site is a useful time line of events in the struggle against segregation.

National Association for Equal Opportunity in Higher Education (www.nafeo.org). Web site of a pro–affirmative action organization that focuses on issues in higher education. The organization works to aid historically black universities and colleges as well as blacks in higher education generally.

The Stanford Encyclopedia of Philosophy: Affirmative Action (http://plato.stanford.edu/entries/affirmative-action). This Web page provides a detailed but succinct history of affirmative action as well as a balanced presentation of some of the ethical issues involved. Especially useful is the bibliography at the end of the article.

Index

DATE DUE
